W9-ATQ-910

Visual Index

16 18 18 20 22 24 26 28 30 32 34 34 34

36 38 40 42 44 46 48 50 50 52 52 54

56 58 60 62 62 64 66 66 68 68 70 72 74

76 78 80 82 84 84 86 86 88 88 88 90 92

92 94 96 96 98 100 102 104 106 108 108 110 112

114 116 116 118 120 120 122 124 124 126 126 128 130

□ BABY COSTUMES

Please see last-minute costumes on pages 133-139.

Illegally Easy™
Halloween Costumes for Kids
100 costumes with simple patterns, no-sew shortcuts,
last-minute solutions, treat bags & accessories

Tikka Books
www.tikkabooks.com

**Illegally Easy™
Halloween Costumes for Kids**
100 costumes with simple patterns, no-sew shortcuts, last-minute solutions, treat bags & accessories
Copyright © 2001, Leila Peltosaari

Published by Tikka Books
P.O. Box 203
Chambly Quebec J3L 4B3 Canada
Phone: (450) 658-6205, Fax: (450) 658-3514
www.tikkabooks.com   leila@tikkabooks.com

Layout and cover: Albert Albala
Production coordinator: Elie Albala
Coloring of line drawings, photo shoot coordinator: Rina Maarit Albala
Photos: Multi-Média, Mark Higden
Pattern digitizing: Hugo Frappier
Makeup: Joëlle Couturier
Illustrations: Marianne Martin
Shoes: Tony Pappas, Montreal

Quantity discounts available for fund-raising and volume purchases.
Printed in Canada on recycled paper.
1 2 3 4 5 6 7 8 9 0

**Other books
by Leila Peltosaari (Leila Albala):**
Easy Sewing for Infants
Easy Sewing for Children
Easy Sewing for Adults
Easy Halloween Costumes for Children
Catalogue of Canadian Catalogues
Hey Kids... Let's Make Gifts!
College Cuisine

National Library of Canada Cataloguing in Publication Data
Peltosaari, Leila, 1947-
         Illegally easy Halloween costumes for kids : 100 costumes with simple patterns, no-sew shortcuts, last-minute solutions, treat bags & accessories

Includes index.
ISBN 1-896106-03-X

         1. Children--Costume. 2. Dressmaking--Patterns. 3. Handicraft. 4. Halloween.
I. Title. II. Title: Halloween costumes for kids.

TT633.P44 2001   646.4'7806   C2001-900492-3

Acknowledgments

The children featured in the photographs are just regular kids with no previous experience with photo shoots. Yet each one rose to the level of a professional model, loving it with patience and good humor. They made my costumes come alive, spontaneously adopting the mood of each character. I am very grateful to these terrific children (and their parents): Maximilien Besner, Tyla Borden, Anne Bovin, Junie Carrière, Eric and Louis-François Charette, Lillian Cheung, Pascal Chiva-Bernard, Gabriel and Laurence Desjardins, Courtney and Stacy Forster-Paris, Maria José and Daniel Godoy, Lars Hefti, Chris and Mathew Higden, Annabelle and Roxanne Laftéchoux, Daniel and Marie-José Poulin, Kendra and Mikayla Ryan, Claudie and Jasmine Sabourin, Emily, Maria Augustina and Sofia Vuletich, Alexy and Anthony Zogheib.

The children in these photos have roots in many corners of the globe: England, Finland, France, Hong Kong, Ireland, Italy, Lebanon, Scotland, Spain, Switzerland, Ukraine, Uruguay, Venezuela, Yugoslavia and, of course, Canada, particularly Quebec, and the Outaouais First Nation in Quebec.

A very special thank you, for being there, for caring, for ideas, and help in many ways, to Elie Albala, Maarit Peltosaari, Margaretha Hefti, Brenda Lee, Norma Sinclair, Sheila Mullin, David Paris, Carolyn Forster-Paris, Odile Rique, Dena Bracken, Julie Sabourin, Geneviève Boisjoly, Beverly Farley, Mary Mulari, Nancy's Notions, and Sylvie Payette.

And to Albert Albala for the cover, well-organized layout, and so much more, Mark and Karen Higden for their humor and hard work with the photographs, Hugo Frappier for digitizing my patterns, Marianne Martin for her charming illustrations, and Joëlle Couturier for the creative makeup on the kids.

And to Maddy Cranley, Alex Procos, Donna Schwerdel, and Michelle West for repeated proofreading and tireless, patient editing.

And finally, for endless reasons, to my daughter, Rina, without whom this book would not have been possible.

I dedicate this book to children everywhere including, of course, my own.

Contents

Traditional Halloween Costumes
8 COSTUMES • PAGES 16 TO 29

Excitement is in the air long before Halloween when the frightful creatures of the dark take center stage for one night. The traditional, always popular Halloween costumes are downright scary, reminding us of the ancient pagan roots behind our joyful, modern celebrations.

Storybook & Fantasy Characters
20 COSTUMES • PAGES 30 TO 61

"Once upon a time in a mysterious, faraway land..." sets the perfect tone for amazing adventures. Magic makes anything possible with aids such as flying carpets, invisible rings, and genie-filled oil lamps.

★ *no-sew costume or no-sew shortcut*

Celestial & Beyond Earth

10 COSTUMES
PAGES 62 TO 77

Long ago the Church sanctified the ancient pagan holiday of Samhain. Religious and spiritual characters were combined with other traditional costumes so that people could continue celebrating the popular customs of their past.

Our vast universe, space travel, as well as the possible existence of alien life, continue to fascinate us and add new dimensions to our life on earth.

Send In the Clowns

7 COSTUMES • PAGES 90 TO 99

Professional clowns emerged in the late Middle Ages when traveling entertainers, imitating the popular court jesters, developed their acts for festival time. Their fame spread and they brought laughter to audiences throughout Europe. Traditionally dressed in outlandish costumes and wacky makeup, clowns entertain us with their juggling, miming, and practical jokes.

Animal Costumes

10 COSTUMES • PAGES 78 TO 89

Warm and cozy outfits bring the animal kingdom to life on Halloween night, all the while keeping trick-or-treaters happy and comfortable.

★ *no-sew costume or no-sew shortcut*

(continues on next page)

Cultural & Historic Tributes

14 COSTUMES • PAGES 100 TO 121

Halloween is a perfect time to dress up in exotic and interesting costumes borrowed from other cultures and eras.

Last-Minute Panic Solutions ★

24 COSTUMES • PAGES 133 TO 139

It's five minutes to Halloween...

Country Costumes

7 COSTUMES • PAGES 122 TO 131

Country images of peaceful nature, golden fields of corn, and colorful autumn trees are the inspirations behind these costumes.

Baby Costumes

AT A GLANCE

★ *no-sew costume or no-sew shortcut*

Let's Celebrate Halloween

Feverish anticipation begins weeks before Halloween as spooky, exciting decorations appear everywhere and children start dreaming about costumes and candies. The magic doesn't come soon enough because, for most kids, Halloween is the only occasion in the whole year when they can disguise themselves. With summer gone and the Christmas season still so far away, Halloween mushrooms into a long celebration at the end of October. This event is no longer for just one brief night. Many teachers encourage children to wear their outfits to school. Costume contests, costumed birthday parties, as well as Halloween parties, are increasingly popular. A good costume or two will see your child through any occasion.

This book brings you an endless source of unique costume ideas for children of all ages. My designs include not only traditional, but also fantasy and storybook characters, celestial and outer space personas, animals, clowns, and country costumes, as well as historic and cultural tributes. Most of these costumes can be made without a sewing machine, including several last-minute panic solutions, so anyone can make them and celebrate Halloween in style.

These comfortable and safe costumes are so easy that you cannot go wrong. The simple grid patterns can be enlarged in minutes, often directly onto the fabric. I will show you shortcuts, suggest easy-to-handle materials, and describe hot glue and fusing methods so that most outfits can be made in just one evening. Some will take only an hour, while a few might take part of your weekend. It's worth every minute of your time.

For less than the price of a flimsy nylon costume and an uncomfortable mask, you can create an unforgettable original for a child. The fabrics, colors, details, and accessories make the costumes appear professional and attractive. A handmade Halloween costume never goes out of style, but will make a comeback year after year for yet another lucky child. If you have a bit of extra time, you might also enjoy creating one of my treat bags to match the costume.

A great costume is not just a disguise used to collect candy. Each character has a little story or intriguing history behind it, exploring folklore, myth, and fact. Encourage your children to develop their creative imagination by letting them choose their own costumes and participate in making them. Stepping outside their everyday world through costumes and role-playing is beneficial to personal development and a healthy alternative to toys, videogames, and passive television viewing.

It's Halloween. It's time for magic and fantasy. Children will never forget a costume made especially for them. Just imagine the memories!

History of Halloween

Halloween may seem custom-made for today's children but, as with most celebrations, it has interesting roots dating back thousands of years. Most symbols and customs of modern Halloween originate from ancient Celtic and Roman festivities.

The Celtic tribes that lived over two thousand years ago in what is now Great Britain and Ireland celebrated their New Year on the first day of November. New Year's Eve was the festival of Samhain, Celtic Lord of Death. The souls of the dead were believed to come to life on that night. Ghosts, goblins, and other creatures of the dark roamed the land. The Celtic priests, known as Druids, went from house to house begging for food and firewood for the festivities. They wore masks and costumes to disguise themselves from evil spirits. Huge bonfires were lit on hilltops. Hearth fires in every home were extinguished and then relit with burning coals carried from the sacred bonfires. Turnips and potatoes were carved into skull-shaped jack-o'-lanterns to safely hold a glowing coal. They were carried door-to-door to light the way for wandering souls and to drive away harmful spirits.

According to Irish legend, the jack-o'-lantern was named after a mean man called Jack. He could not enter heaven because he was too wicked and was barred from hell because he had played tricks on the devil. So poor Jack was condemned to walk the earth as a lost soul with only a lantern to light his way until Judgment Day.

When the Romans conquered Britain in the first century A.D., they regarded the Samhain holiday as barbaric. In an attempt to civilize it by substituting some of their own celebrations, they combined their autumn festival with the festival of Samhain. The Celtic harvest traditions of bonfires, parades, and lanterns were adopted by the Romans and, centuries later, Christians adopted the Roman celebrations. In the eighth century, to rid the already popular harvest festival of its pagan elements, the Church established All Hallows' Day (All Saints' Day) on November 1. This sanctified the ancient holiday and the people could keep the customs they had celebrated before becoming Christians. In medieval times, elaborately dressed statues of saints were paraded through the streets while parishioners dressed up as saints and biblical characters. Many of the traditional Celtic customs survived and continued to be celebrated on "Hallows' Eve".

Brought to North America by a great wave of Irish and Scottish immigrants in the 19th century, Hallows' Eve became Hallowe'en and evolved into an occasion for hayrides, bonfires, ghost stories, and practical jokes. Gradually this festive day became what we now celebrate as Halloween. Many communities sponsor dances, costume parades, contests, and other celebrations. Pumpkins have replaced Irish turnips for jack-o'-lanterns, while costumes and trick-or-treating remain as humorous reminders of ancient ghoulish traditions.

Trick-or-treat for UNICEF

What started as a small gesture by a few concerned children has grown to become one of the mainstays of the UNICEF fund-raising programs in the United States and Canada. It all started in 1950, when a small Sunday school class in the U.S. decided to collect money for needy children, instead of asking for candy on Halloween. They donated their check, totaling $17, to UNICEF (United Nations Children's Fund). Since then, the programs have raised over $200 million.

Individuals, groups, organizations, educational institutions, and corporations have all contributed to this wonderful North American tradition of children helping children less fortunate than themselves. These funds help needy children to have access to good nutrition, clean water, immunization, health care, education, and basic human rights.

Millions of grade school children participate in the "Trick-or-Treat for UNICEF" campaign by carrying the familiar orange UNICEF boxes. Junior and senior high school students support the program through various fund-raising activities. Retailers and businesses raise money through the large counter-box program. Numerous special events not only celebrate the spirit of Halloween, but also raise valuable funds for those in need.

You can learn more about this campaign or lend your support by visiting the UNICEF web sites at:

- www.unicefusa.org
- www.unicef.ca

unicef
United Nations Children's Fund

A portion of the proceeds from the sale of this book will be donated to UNICEF. Thank you on behalf of the children of the world.

Make Halloween Safe

Trick-or-treat in groups or with an adult. Keep in mind these golden rules for a safe Halloween.

Approach only houses that signal a welcome.

Carry only harmless props.

Inspect the treats carefully.

Be visible in the dark.

Map out your route.

Wear makeup instead of a mask.

Wear comfortable shoes.

Respect traffic rules. Cross the street only at corners.

General Instructions

Child's choice

Consider your time and budget but, most importantly, respect your child's choice. Any gender reference is usually coincidental since most costumes are appropriate for both boys and girls. Let the kids help. They love to be creative and will enjoy designing their own secret crests, treasure maps, or treat bags. They do not expect perfect results. Thrilled with anticipation, they simply want to have fun.

Pattern sizes

Size	Small	Medium	Large
Approximate age in years	3-4	6-8	10-12
Imperial, height inches (")	37-42	47-52	56-61
Imperial, chest inches (")	21-23	25-27	29-30
Metric, height cm	94-107	120-132	142-155
Metric, chest cm	53-58	64-69	74-76

Adjust the pattern, if necessary, before cutting out the fabric. This book includes both imperial and metric measurements, rounded off for ease of use; the slight differences between the two systems are irrelevant. Most patterns are so simple that you can safely enlarge or reduce the size with flexible accuracy.

Enlarging grid patterns

Enlarging grid patterns is so easy that children can do it. Each side of a square equals one inch (2.5cm). Basic patterns are used for several costumes, so they are shown only once and then cross-referenced on other pages.

Enlarge the easiest patterns directly onto a large sheet of any paper. Using a measuring tape, measure and mark all corner points of the pattern on the paper. Then draw the full-size pattern by connecting the points with lines as shown.

Some patterns are so simple that you can enlarge them directly onto the fabric.

To enlarge a pattern with more details, use a cardboard cutting board with a grid printed on it. Tape a sheet of tracing paper or gift tissue on top. Enlarge the pattern to the full-size grid by marking all corners and then connecting them with lines as shown. Or use one-inch (2.5cm) grid paper.

Consider using a photocopy machine to enlarge the smallest, most intricate patterns like the tiara or crown.

Or simply use a pattern just as a general inspiration and make your own version.

Supplies to enlarge grid patterns

These are not listed separately for each costume. You'll need:
- ❑ measuring tape
- ❑ paper*
- ❑ pen
- ❑ scissors

*Depending on the pattern, use sheets of newspaper, brown paper, tissue paper, or grid paper.

(continues on next page)

Simple directions,
no-sew shortcuts, cutting the fabric

My directions are short and simple with color-coded patterns and a list of supplies for easy reference. Regard these ideas and patterns as an inspiration rather than as an absolute blueprint. Write down everything you need for a costume or take this book with you to the store.

Most of these costumes can be made without a sewing machine, or by using suggested no-sew shortcuts (see no-sew icon, page 15). For others, any ordinary sewing machine will be sufficient, with just a basic sewing knowledge necessary.

When two pieces are required, cut the pattern from folded fabric so the pieces will automatically be mirror images of each other.

Pin all the required pattern pieces to wrong side of fabric before you cut them out. Unless specified, sew seams with right sides of fabric together.

Seam allowances, fabric requirements, special occasion fabrics

The patterns include seam allowances of 3/8" (1cm) and hem allowances of 1-2" (2.5cm - 5cm). I have compiled fabric and notion requirements for each costume. Feel free to take artistic liberty and use fabrics and colors of your choice.

Special occasion fabrics fascinate kids. Consider using them especially for indoor costumes. Fancy fabrics such as taffeta, organza, velvet, lurex, or satin are often available at discount prices or in remnant bins. Look beyond common alternatives to make the costume special. Even humble fabrics like an old sheet or curtain and inexpensive broadcloth can look extraordinary when trimmed with ribbons, gold glitter, and other decorative details.

Polarfleece, arctic fleece, polyester fleece, polar, fleece, high loft fleece

Polarfleece® is a registered trademark of Malden Mills for arctic fleece or polyester fleece (also known as polar, fleece, and high loft fleece). Since the word Polarfleece has become so well-known that, although incorrect, it is commonly used generically, I have used that term in this book. Polarfleece is the easiest and most perfect fabric for children's Halloween costumes, especially for cold nights of trick-or-treating. It is soft and lightweight, slightly stretchy, easy-care and durable, warm and comfortable. It hotglues well, is conveniently wide, and relatively inexpensive. It doesn't run, ravel, or shrink, and no hemming or seam finishing is needed when making quick costumes and accessories. It is available almost everywhere these days in dozens of solid colors and prints. **Determine the right side with this stretch test**: When stretched, Polarfleece curls to the wrong side across the width on the cross-grain.

When lightweight, soft flexibility is not essential, consider using felt for costumes such as Snowman, Bat, Ladybug, and Pumpkin, or for accessories and trimmings.

Hot glue gun and glue sticks, safety precautions

Available in hardware and craft stores, a hot glue gun is a handy tool for making costumes and especially useful for Polarfleece fabrics and many accessories. Just plug it in, insert a glue stick and within minutes, you can glue almost anything together quickly and easily. Test on scrap fabrics first. Hot glue bonds items almost immediately. After it has cooled, pull off any stray glue strings.

Protect your working surface by using newspapers or a Polarfleece scrap to catch drips. Never leave a hot glue gun unattended. Always keep it away from children and pets. Hot glue and the hot glue gun are extremely hot and can burn you or your child if you are not careful. Keep a bowl of ice water nearby in case of accidental burns. When practical, protect your hands by using tweezers or Polarfleece scraps or by wearing gloves. Always allow the hotglued items time to completely cool before your child puts on the costume. **Never hotglue anything onto the costume while your child is wearing it.**

Velcro

Velcro® is a registered trademark for hook-and-loop fastener tape. It comes with one tape of dense nylon hooks and another tape of dense nylon pile that interlock firmly when pressed together. It is fast and practical as a closure for helmets, tabard sides, and belts instead of buttons, zippers, snaps, ties, etc.

Fusible web and paper-backed fusible web

Fusible web is a translucent mesh fabric adhesive, sold at fabric stores by the yard (or meter). Bond thin fabrics by placing fusible web between two layers and pressing with a medium-hot iron. You can even fuse foil or gift wrap on a posterboard. Also use fusible web to seal a wire frame between two fabric layers to make wings. Make quick hems with a strip of fusible web. Ready-made web strip is also available.

Paper-backed fusible web is handy for two-step fusing of even the smallest and most intricate designs. First draw the design on the paper side as a mirror image of the final design. Iron it to the wrong side of appliqué fabric with paper against the iron. Cut out the design and peel off the paper. Place the design on the right side of garment, cover with press cloth, and press with a medium-hot iron. For best results, always read the manufacturer's instruction sheet and test on scrap fabrics first. Use paper-backed fusible web for jobs like decorating the Dracula bag or fusing stars and moons on the Wizard costume.

Do not touch fusible web directly with a hot iron or it will melt. Protect the fabric and iron with a press cloth or sheet of paper. When the iron is cold, clean off any fusible web residue with a cotton ball dipped in nail polish remover. Paper-backed fusible web is generally used to position appliqués securely so that you can zigzag the edges neatly in place. Both webs are perfect no-sew shortcuts for many costumes.

Marks used in patterns

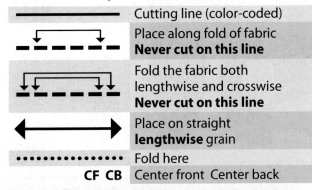

————————	Cutting line (color-coded)
↓ ↓ (dashed)	Place along fold of fabric **Never cut on this line**
↓ ↓ (dashed)	Fold the fabric both lengthwise and crosswise **Never cut on this line**
←——————→	Place on straight **lengthwise** grain
••••••••••••	Fold here
CF CB	Center front Center back

No-sew costumes and no-sew shortcuts are marked with a star on pages 6-8. ★
The no-sew icon shown here signals a no-sew shortcut on costume pages (some hand-sewing may be needed). A sewing machine is included in the supply list of those costumes that absolutely require one.

Dracula

Frightening vampires leave their graves and coffins at night to disturb the living and suck their blood. The legendary Dracula, the classiest and most popular of all vampires, immortalized in many movies, fascinates kids and adults of all ages, especially during Halloween.

CAPE

With right sides together, stitch center back and side seams of fabric and lining separately. Stitch lining to cape, leaving neck edge open. Trim corners, turn right side out, and press. Place interfacing on wrong side of collar. Stitch collar to lining, leaving neck edge open. Trim corners, clip curves, turn right side out, and press. Gather neck edge of the cape and stitch the collar to the cape. Sew ties from leftover fabric and stitch to front edge below collar.

SMART SHORTCUT

Just make a gorgeous cape. Wear dark pants, mom's pretty blouse, and a long scarf for a sash.

WHAT YOU NEED

Size (approximate age in years)→	Small (3-4)	Medium (6-8)	Large (10-12)
Black taffeta or similar fabric for cape and treat bag, 55" (140cm) wide:	1½ yds. (1.40m)	2¼ yds. (2.10m)	2¾ yds. (2.60m)
Red lining satin for cape lining and sash, 55" (140cm) wide:	1½ yds. (1.40m)	2¼ yds. (2.10m)	2¾ yds. (2.60m)
Black Polarfleece for pants, 60" (150cm) wide:	⅞ yd. (0.80m)	1 yd. (1.00m)	1¼ yds. (1.20m)
White fabric for shirt, 45" (115cm) wide:	1½ yds. (1.40m)	2¼ yds. (2.10m)	2½ yds. (2.30m)
Lace for shirt neck, front, and sleeve ends:	3½ yds. (3.10m)	4 yds. (3.50m)	4½ yds. (4.00m)

Other supplies: ❑ stiff interfacing for cape collar ❑ wide elastic for waist **For treat bag:** ❑ fabric for lining
❑ bias binding for shirt neck edge ❑ sewing machine ❑ paper-backed fusible web
❑ narrow elastic for shirt neck and sleeve ends ❑ fabric scraps for decorations

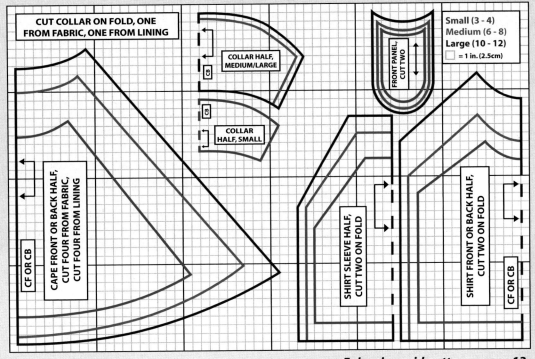

CUT COLLAR ON FOLD, ONE FROM FABRIC, ONE FROM LINING

COLLAR HALF, MEDIUM/LARGE

CB

CB

COLLAR HALF, SMALL

FRONT PANEL, CUT TWO

Small (3 - 4)
Medium (6 - 8)
Large (10 - 12)
☐ = 1 in. (2.5cm)

CAPE FRONT OR BACK HALF, CUT FOUR FROM FABRIC, CUT FOUR FROM LINING

CF OR CB

SHIRT SLEEVE HALF, CUT TWO ON FOLD

SHIRT FRONT OR BACK HALF, CUT TWO ON FOLD

CF OR CB

Enlarging grid patterns, page 13.

SHIRT

Stitch sleeves to bodice. Stitch sides and underarms. Hem lower edge. Trim sleeve ends with lace. On inside, stitch stretched elastic around wrists to make ruffles. Sew bias binding around neck edge to make a casing and insert narrow elastic. Sew the front panel double-layered, add rows of gathered lace on top, and then sew the panel to shirt front. Stitch lace around neck, stretching the elasticized edge as you sew.

PANTS
Pattern, page 21.

SHIRRED SASH

Cut a piece of red lining satin, about 20" x 55" (50cm x 140cm). Machine-baste several vertical lines across width. Pull upper threads to gather the fabric and tie thread ends securely together. Fold in half lengthwise and stitch the side seam. Turn right side out. Stitch ends closed. Tie around waist.

TREAT BAG
Pattern, page 71.

Line the bag if you make it from taffeta or other thin fabric. Iron paper-backed fusible web to the wrong side of fabric scraps. Cut out images of a tree, tombstone, bat, and moon. Peel off the backing paper and iron the images onto the bag. Draw details on tombstone with a black marker.

Ghost & Mummy

Ghosts, the spirits of the dead, return to the world of the living on Halloween night. They wander among the excited trick-or-treaters, scaring everyone with their shadowy images. Befitting the spooky Halloween legend, a mummy is a dead body that is thousands of years old. The ancient Egyptian process of mummification preserved the body with treatments of resin, balsamic oils, and careful wrapping in linen bandages.

ghost costume

 **BALACLAVA HELMET**
Pattern, page 55.

 **NO-SEW SHORTCUT**
Hotglue the seams.

HOODED ROBE
Stitch sides and underarms. Cut sleeve ends as shown. Stitch top and back seam of hood. Stitch hood around neck opening.

SAFETY TIP
For a small child, cut the robe short enough to prevent tripping.

 **MITTENS**
from Polarfleece.
Pattern, page 49.

 **TREAT BAG**
Pattern, page 71.
Decorate the bag with two ghosts framed by a window pane and orange curtains, all cut from scrap fabrics and hotglued in place.

WHAT YOU NEED

Size (approximate age in years)→	Small (3-4)	Medium (6-8)	Large (10-12)
Ghost: White Polarfleece for hooded robe, mittens, and balaclava helmet, 60" (150cm) wide:	2 yds. (1.80m)	2½ yds. (2.30m)	2¾ yds. (2.60m)

Mummy:
❑ white fabric for bandages, 2-3 yds. (2.00m - 3.00m), or an old sheet
❑ old sweatsuit   ❑ lots of safety pins   ❑ hot glue gun and glue sticks

Both treat bags:
❑ black Polarfleece and fabric scraps
❑ hot glue gun and glue sticks

mummy costume

COSTUME

Twist the white fabric and dip briefly in cooled strong tea for uneven stains. Let dry. Stuff an old sweatsuit with crumpled newspaper. Cut the fabric into wide strips. Wrap and hotglue the strips loosely all around the sweatsuit, top and bottom separately. Remove the newspaper. Put the sweatsuit on the child. Wrap child's head, hands, and feet, and attach loose ends with safety pins.

TREAT BAG

Stitch the side seam. Pin the bottom circle to the bag and stitch. Cut holes around top edge. Cut a long strip from leftover fabric and weave it through the holes for a drawstring.
From fabric scraps, cut out fancy bottle shapes and hotglue to the bag.

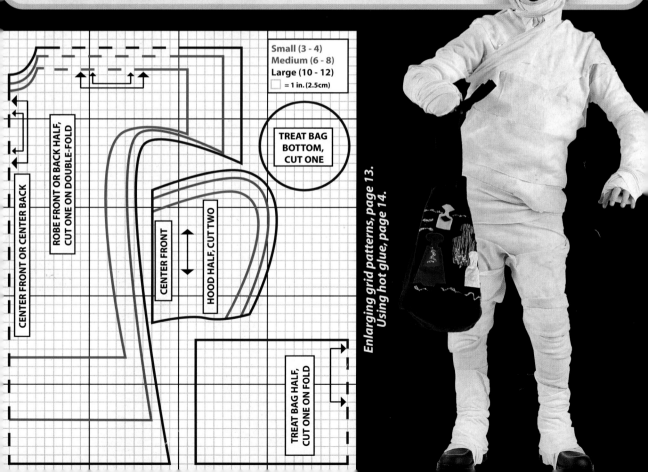

Small (3 - 4)
Medium (6 - 8)
Large (10 - 12)
☐ = 1 in. (2.5cm)

CENTER FRONT OR CENTER BACK

ROBE FRONT OR BACK HALF, CUT ONE ON DOUBLE-FOLD

CENTER FRONT

HOOD HALF, CUT TWO

TREAT BAG BOTTOM, CUT ONE

TREAT BAG HALF, CUT ONE ON FOLD

Enlarging grid patterns, page 13.
Using hot glue, page 14.

Skeleton

The night before the ancient Celts celebrated the first day of winter and darkness, frightening creatures came to life. A spooky gang of skeletons is ready to scare everyone silly and cast a delightful gloom over the celebrations.

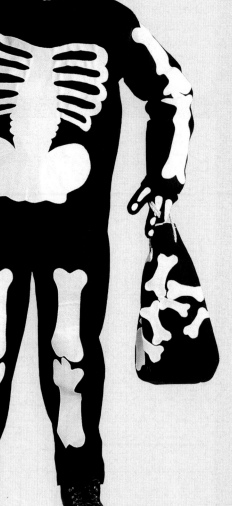

BALACLAVA HELMET
Pattern, page 55.

TOP AND PANTS

Stitch shoulder seams of top. Stitch sleeves to bodice. Stitch sides and under-arms. Pin pants front to back. Stitch inner leg seams. Stitch center seam. Stitch side seams. Stitch waist edge under into a casing and insert elastic.

GLOVES FROM POLARFLEECE
See Astronaut, page 77.

TREAT BAG
Pattern, page 19.

Cut small bone shapes from white Polarfleece scraps and hotglue all over the bag. (Sneaky shortcut: Use self-adhesive vinyl for bones.)

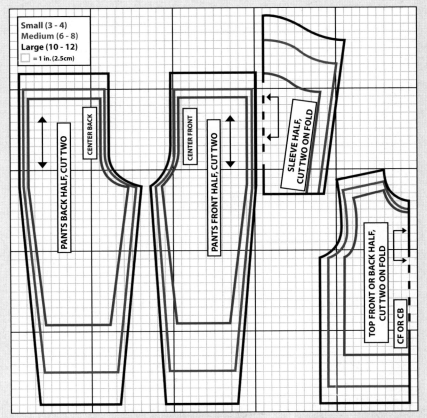

Small (3 - 4)
Medium (6 - 8)
Large (10 - 12)
☐ = 1 in. (2.5cm)

PANTS BACK HALF, CUT TWO

CENTER BACK

CENTER FRONT

PANTS FRONT HALF, CUT TWO

SLEEVE HALF, CUT TWO ON FOLD

TOP FRONT OR BACK HALF, CUT TWO ON FOLD

CF OR CB

Enlarging grid patterns, page 13. Using hot glue, page 14.

FINAL TOUCH

Draw simple bones on the paper backing of self-adhesive vinyl, cut out, peel the backing off, and apply onto the costume as shown. Cut small bone shapes from white Polarfleece scraps and hotglue to glove fingers.

NO-SEW SHORTCUT

Wear a black sweatsuit turned inside out to hide any decorative details. Trim temporarily with self-adhesive vinyl cut into bones as shown. Balaclava helmet can be hotglued together (or use a white scarf). Buy stretchy mini-gloves and trim with bones cut from self-adhesive vinyl.

WHAT YOU NEED

Size (approximate age in years)→	Small (3-4)	Medium (6-8)	Large (10-12)
White Polarfleece for balaclava helmet, 60" (150cm) wide:	½ yd. (0.50m)	½ yd. (0.50m)	½ yd. (0.50m)
Black Polarfleece for top, pants, gloves, and pouch, 60" (150cm) wide:	1¾ yds. (1.60m)	2½ yds. (2.30m)	3 yds. (2.70m)
White, self-adhesive vinyl for bone decorations, 17" (43cm) wide:	1¼ yds. (1.20m)	1¾ yds. (1.60m)	2 yds. (1.80m)

Other supplies: ☐ wide elastic for waist ☐ hot glue gun and glue sticks

Devil

The devil, a symbol of evil and demonic spirits, reminds us of the traditional characters of old pagan festivals.

HELMET

Pattern, page 101.

Stitch sides of horns, stuff with fabric scraps, and handsew to the helmet.

CAPE

Stitch center back and side seams. Line one collar with interfacing. Stitch collars together, leaving neck egde open. Trim corners, clip curves, and turn right side out. Gather neck edge of cape and stitch the collar to the cape. From leftover fabric, sew a tab and add Velcro for closure under collar. Cut out orange and yellow flame images and hotglue to the cape.

WARNING

Do not use red makeup around eyes.

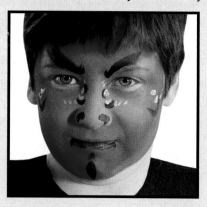

WHAT YOU NEED

Size (approximate age in years)→	Small (3-4)	Medium (6-8)	Large (10-12)
Red Polarfleece for cape, tail, helmet, and cauldron, 60" (150cm) wide:	2 yds. (1.80m)	2¾ yds. (2.60m)	3 yds. (2.70m)

Other supplies:
- ❑ small piece of Velcro for helmet and cape closure
- ❑ hot glue gun and glue sticks
- ❑ orange and yellow Polarfleece or felt pieces for flame decorations
- ❑ medium-weight, non-fusible interfacing for collar
- ❑ plastic cauldron
- ❑ one safety pin

TAIL

Roll up a long piece of red Polarfleece for a tail and hotglue closed. Cut two large triangles from red Polarfleece and hotglue together on two sides. Stuff with fabric scraps and glue the tail end inside. Pin the other end to the back of the pants.

NO-SEW SHORTCUT

Make a balaclava helmet, page 55. Hotglue everything. Hotglue ties under collar front.

TREAT CONTAINER

Hotglue red Polarfleece around a plastic cauldron and handle. Decorate with flame images to match the cape.

Enlarging grid patterns, page 13. Using hot glue, page 14.

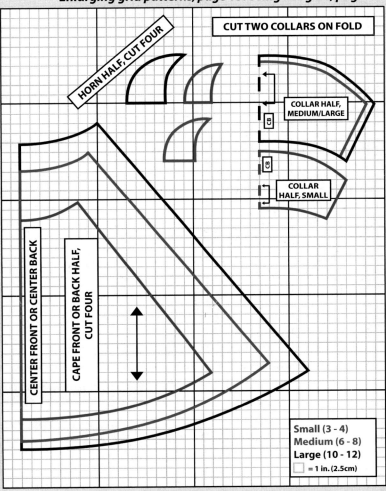

HORN HALF, CUT FOUR

CUT TWO COLLARS ON FOLD

COLLAR HALF, MEDIUM/LARGE

CB

CB

COLLAR HALF, SMALL

CENTER FRONT OR CENTER BACK

CAPE FRONT OR BACK HALF, CUT FOUR

Small (3 - 4)
Medium (6 - 8)
Large (10 - 12)
❑ = 1 in. (2.5cm)

Halloween Witch

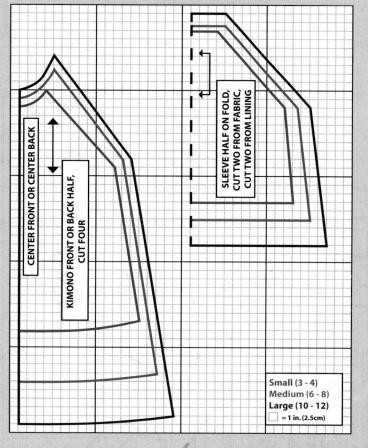

CENTER FRONT OR CENTER BACK

KIMONO FRONT OR BACK HALF, CUT FOUR

SLEEVE HALF ON FOLD, CUT TWO FROM FABRIC, CUT TWO FROM LINING

Small (3 - 4)
Medium (6 - 8)
Large (10 - 12)
☐ = 1 in. (2.5cm)

Every Halloween, seemingly ordinary humans turn into friendly witches. With a trusted black cat for a companion, they concoct magic spells and alluring treats for children.

KIMONO

With wrong sides together, stitch orange lining to sleeves at lower edge and then treat layers as one. Stitch center back seam. Stitch sleeves to bodice. Stitch sides and underarms. Gather neck edge for a comfortable fit. Cut a long strip from leftover fabric, press in half, and stitch around neck edge with ends extending into ties.

Enlarging grid patterns, page 13.
Using hot glue, page 14.

WHAT YOU NEED

Size (approximate age in years)→	Small (3-4)	Medium (6-8)	Large (10-12)
Black Polarfleece for kimono and hat, 60" (150cm) wide:	2 yds. (1.80m)	2½ yds. (2.30m)	3 yds. (2.70m)
Orange broadcloth or flannelette for gown, hat, and sleeve linings, 45" (115cm) wide:	3 yds. (2.70m)	4¼ yds. (3.90m)	4¾ yds. (4.30m)

Other supplies:
☐ nylon witch hat
☐ paper-backed fusible web for decoration
☐ wide bias binding for gown neck edge
☐ elastic for neck opening
☐ large plastic cauldron
☐ hot glue gun and glue sticks
☐ sewing machine

HAT

Start with a ready-made nylon witch hat. Hotglue black fabric around crown and orange fabric under brim. Cut a strip from orange fabric and tie it on for a ribbon as shown.

 **GOWN**
Pattern, page 127.

FINAL TOUCH

Iron paper-backed fusible web to the wrong side of fabric scraps. Cut out a black cat, fence, and a large orange moon. Peel off the paper and iron the decorative pieces onto front as shown.

WARM TOUCH
(Not shown in photo.)

Sew neck warmer and arm warmers from black Polarfleece, see page 30.

TREAT CONTAINER
is a plastic cauldron.

Common Witch

After carefully selecting ancient spells from the Book of Shadows, witches brew magic potions in their black cauldrons. The traditional witches fly across the midnight sky and cast magic upon unsuspecting mortals.

HAIR

Cut hair from green Polarfleece. Cut one long edge into a narrow fringe and pull into curls. Hotglue the uncut edge to the inside of the hat. Trim as desired.

SLEEVELESS DRESS

Stitch shoulders and side seams. Cut hem as shown.

KIMONO

Stitch center back seam. Stitch shoulder seams. Stitch sides and underarms. Cut hem and sleeve ends as shown.

CAT PENDANT

Hotglue black felt to cardboard. Cut out a simple cat image and decorate as desired. Make a hook from a paper clip and attach the pendant to a long ribbon.

WHAT YOU NEED

Size (approximate age in years)→	Small (3-4)	Medium (6-8)	Large (10-12)
Green broadcloth for dress, 45" (115cm) wide:	¾ yd. (0.70m)	1⅞ yds. (1.80m)	2⅛ yds. (2.00m)
Black broadcloth for kimono, 45" (115cm) wide:	1½ yds. (1.40m)	2¼ yds. (2.10m)	2½ yds. (2.30m)

Other supplies:
❑ nylon witch hat ❑ hot glue gun and glue sticks
❑ green Polarfleece for hair,
    20" long x 10" wide (50cm long x 25cm wide)

For pendant:
❑ black felt scrap ❑ stiff cardboard ❑ paper clip
❑ ribbon ❑ craft supplies for decorations
❑ hot glue gun and glue sticks

NO-SEW VERSION

The seams can be handsewn or hotglued.

PATTERNLESS TREAT BAG

Sew pieces of leftover fabric together into a large circle. Cut holes around edge. Cut a long strip from leftover fabric, weave it through the holes for a drawstring, and knot ends together.

Enlarging grid patterns, page 13. Using hot glue, page 14.

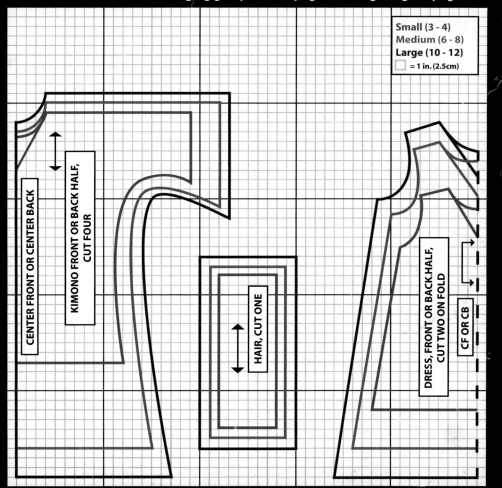

Small (3 - 4)
Medium (6 - 8)
Large (10 - 12)
☐ = 1 in. (2.5cm)

CENTER FRONT OR CENTER BACK

KIMONO FRONT OR BACK HALF, CUT FOUR

HAIR, CUT ONE

DRESS, FRONT OR BACK HALF, CUT TWO ON FOLD

CF OR CB

Frankenstein's Monster

Made famous in many movies based on the popular novel, Frankenstein's monster continues to intrigue and terrify us. Victor Frankenstein is the original "mad scientist" whose fascinating monster is a legendary experiment gone wrong. The scientist creates an artificial man from bits and pieces of corpses and, using powerful jolts of electricity, brings his experiment to life. The result is a monster who seeks affection but is so ugly and repulsive that he frightens everyone. Lonely and miserable, he loses his mind and eventually kills his creator.

Enlarging grid patterns, page 13. Using hot glue, page 14.

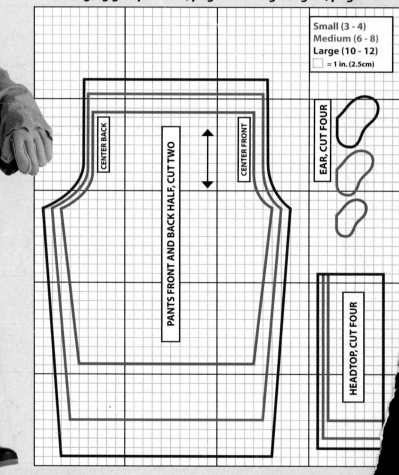

Small (3 - 4)
Medium (6 - 8)
Large (10 - 12)
☐ = 1 in. (2.5cm)

CENTER BACK

PANTS FRONT AND BACK HALF, CUT TWO

CENTER FRONT

EAR, CUT FOUR

HEADTOP, CUT FOUR

WHAT YOU NEED

Size (approximate age in years)	Small (3-4)	Medium (6-8)	Large (10-12)
Medium-weight cotton-type fabric for pants, jacket, and treat bag, 55" (140cm) wide:	2¼ yds. (2.10m)	2¾ yds. (2.60m)	3⅛ yds. (2.90m)
Green Polarfleece for helmet, ears, and gloves, 60" (150cm) wide:	¾ yd. (0.70m)	¾ yd. (0.70m)	¾ yd. (0.70m)
Black Polarfleece or felt for headtop, 60" (150cm) wide:	¼ yd. (0.25m)	¼ yd. (0.25m)	¼ yd. (0.25m)

Other supplies:
- ❑ 3 or 4 large buttons
- ❑ square (about 6-7" or 15cm - 18cm) of thick foam or stiff cardboard for headtop
- ❑ hot glue gun and glue sticks
- ❑ elastic or cord for waist
- ❑ corks, spirals, and screws
- ❑ black permanent marker
- ❑ small piece of Velcro for helmet

HELMET
Pattern, page 101.

Cut the ears from green Polarfleece and hotglue double-layered, stuffing with fabric scraps. Hotglue the ears to the helmet sides. Hotglue corks and screws to the helmet neck.

SQUARE HEADTOP AND HAIR
from black Polarfleece.

Hotglue the headtop pieces to a square piece of foam or cardboard, centering front-to-back and side-to-side, crisscrossing, with fabric ends falling freely. Trim to desired length and cut ends into ragged hair. Hotglue to the helmet.

PANTS

Stitch inner leg seams. Turn one leg right side out and push it into the other leg. Stitch center seam. Turn pants right side out. Cut holes around waist. Weave elastic or drawstring cord through the holes.

JACKET
Pattern, page 123.

Cut unfinished hem and sleeve ends clumsily and unevenly. Draw large mock basting stitches with a black marker over the seams.

GLOVES
See Astronaut, page 77.

 **NO-SEW SHORTCUT**

Use a man's old, baggy suit and work gloves. Make a no-sew balaclava helmet, pattern on page 55, and hotglue the seams. Add ears and headtop as shown.

TREAT BAG
Pattern, page 19.

Fold upper edge under and stitch to form a casing. Cut a long strip from leftover fabric and insert it through casing for a drawstring. Hotglue corks and spirals all over the bag for spare parts.

Wizard

A wizard is a clever sorcerer with mystical, supernatural powers and refined skills. He casts spells with a wave of his hand and uses mysterious objects to produce magic.

CONE HAT

Iron paper-backed fusible web to the wrong side of yellow fabric. Cut out stars and moons. Peel off the paper and iron the images onto the hat before stitching the side seam. Stitch the side seam, fabric and interfacing separately. Turn the fabric hat right side out and slip over interfacing. Topstitch the rims together. Roll up a piece of gold fabric around fiberfill to make a soft band. Hotglue ends together and wrap the band with ribbon. Slip the band over cone hat for a brim. For a chinstrap, cut a tiny hole at each side near lower edge, push elastic through holes, and knot securely.

LONG ROBE
Pattern, page 19 (without hood).

Cut lining for sleeves up to neck edge. With right sides together, stitch lining to sleeves at lower edge. Stitch sides and underarms of robe and lining in one seam, turn right side out, and press. Pin or baste neck edge to lining. Slit neck back for easy fit. Trim raw neck edge and the slit edges with bias binding, extending the ends to tie at back. Press hem under and fuse in place. Decorate the robe with stars and moons to match the hat.

NECK WARMER AND ARM WARMERS
from Polarfleece.

Stitch sides of neck warmer (shown). For wrist-to-elbow arm warmers, sew narrow tubes (not shown).

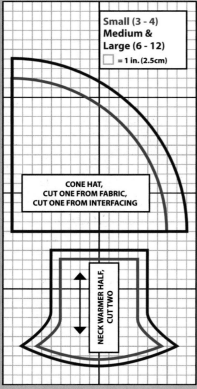

Small (3 - 4)
Medium &
Large (6 - 12)
☐ = 1 in. (2.5cm)

CONE HAT,
CUT ONE FROM FABRIC,
CUT ONE FROM INTERFACING

NECK WARMER HALF,
CUT TWO

Enlarging grid patterns, page 13.
Using hot glue, page 14.

MOON PENDANT

Cut a large moon from stiff cardboard. Brush it with white liquid glue and, while the glue is wet, sprinkle with gold glitter. Punch a hole and attach a long ribbon.

STAFF

Wrap a wooden rod with decorative ribbons and hotglue. Paint a styrofoam ball with poster paints, brush with glue, and add glitter. Punch a hole in the ball and glue the rod end inside.

SAFETY TIP

For a small child, cut the robe short enough to prevent tripping.

NO-SEW SHORTCUT

Make the robe and double-layered hat from Polarfleece. Hotglue all seams. Cut stars and moons from yellow Polarfleece and hotglue to the robe and hat.

TREAT CONTAINER

Cover a plastic pumpkin first with Polarfleece and then with gold metallic fabric, hotgluing all in place.

WHAT YOU NEED

Size (approximate age in years)→	Small (3-4)	Medium (6-8)	Large (10-12)
Purple taffeta, velveteen, or similar for robe and cone hat, 55" (140cm) wide:	2 yds. (1.80m)	3 yds. (2.70m)	3⅛ yds. (2.90m)
Yellow taffeta, velveteen, or similar for sleeve lining and decorations, 55" (140cm) wide:	1 yd. (1.00m)	1 yd. (1.00m)	1 yd. (1.00m)
Paper-backed fusible web for decorations, 13" (33cm) wide:	1 yd. (1.00m)	1 yd. (1.00m)	1 yd. (1.00m)
Stiff, non-fusible interfacing for hat, 18" (46cm) wide:	½ yd. (0.50m)	½ yd. (0.50m)	½ yd. (0.50m)

Other supplies:
❑ bias binding for neck edge and ties
❑ fusible web strip for hem
❑ gold fabric, polyester fiberfill, and decorative ribbon for hat brim
❑ narrow elastic for chinstrap
❑ long cord for waist

For moon pendant and staff:
❑ stiff cardboard
❑ white liquid glue
❑ gold glitter
❑ hot glue gun & glue sticks
❑ wooden rod
❑ ribbons
❑ styrofoam ball
❑ poster paints

For treat container:
❑ plastic pumpkin
❑ Polarfleece
❑ gold fabric
❑ hot glue gun and glue sticks

Optional:
❑ Polarfleece for neck warmer and arm warmers, ⅓ yd. of 60" wide (0.30m of 150cm wide)

Aladdin

Aladdin is a hero in one of the beloved stories of *The Thousand and One Nights,* a collection of Eastern folk tales dating from the tenth century. Aladdin outwits a wicked sorcerer, finds a magic lamp and, by rubbing it, summons a powerful genie who will grant his every wish.

TURBAN

Cut a piece of Polarfleece for lining, 23 (24, 25)" or 58 (61, 64)cm square. Stitch the opposite, non-stretchy edges together into a tube. Roll up lower edge into a soft band and hotglue closed. Slit top edge into six points, taper and hotglue, overlapping as needed, for a round headtop. Drape with fancy fabric and hotglue or handsew in place.

NO-SEW TURBAN

Tape or pin pleated gift wrap or scarf over a hat.

BROOCH

Hotglue fabric to cardboard. Cut out a circle. Decorate with fabric scraps, ribbons, and a fake gem, all hotglued. Hotglue the brooch to the turban front over a feather.

WHAT YOU NEED

Size (approximate age in years)→	Small (3-4)	Medium (6-8)	Large (10-12)
Polarfleece for turban lining and sash padding: 60" (150cm) wide:	¾ yd. (0.70m)	¾ yd. (0.70m)	¾ yd. (0.70m)
Fancy fabric for turban, 45" (115cm) wide:	½ yd. (0.50m)	½ yd. (0.50m)	½ yd. (0.50m)
Fabric for shirt, 45" (115cm) wide:	1½ yds. (1.40m)	2¼ yds. (2.10m)	2½ yds. (2.30m)
Fabric for vest, 45" (115cm) wide:	½ yd. (0.50m)	⅝ yd. (0.60m)	¾ yd. (0.70m)
Fabric for vest lining, 45" (115cm) wide:	½ yd. (0.50m)	⅝ yd. (0.60m)	¾ yd. (0.70m)
Fancy fabric for sash, 45" (115cm) wide:	⅜ yd. (0.40m)	⅜ yd. (0.40m)	⅜ yd. (0.40m)
Fabric for pants, 45" (115cm) wide:	1¼ yds. (1.20m)	2½ yds. (2.30m)	2¾ yds. (2.60m)
Fabric for spats, 45" (115cm) wide:	⅜ yd. (0.40m)	¾ yd. (0.70m)	⅞ yd. (0.80m)

Other supplies:
- ❏ bias binding for neck opening and sleeve ends
- ❏ narrow elastic for shirt neck, sleeve ends, leg ends, and spats
- ❏ wide elastic for waist   ❏ stiff, fusible interfacing for spats
- ❏ sewing machine   ❏ needle and thread   ❏ hot glue gun and glue sticks

For brooch:
- ❏ stiff cardboard
- ❏ fabric scraps
- ❏ ribbons
- ❏ fake gem   ❏ feather

For treat bag:
- ❏ black fabric
- ❏ fancy fabric scraps
- ❏ paper-backed fusible web

SHIRT

Pattern, page 17
(without lacy front panel).

Stitch bias binding around neck edge and sleeve ends to make casings and insert elastic.

VEST

Pattern, page 107.

SQUARE PANTS

Slit seam allowances where shown. Stitch inner leg seams from leg ends up to the slits. With folded edge at crotch, stitch the center panel between side sections, front and back, breaking the stitch at slits. Sew waist edge and leg ends under into casings and insert elastic.

SPATS

Pattern, page 43.

Cut two spats. Iron interfacing to the wrong side. Stitch seams. For a strap under shoe, sew a piece of elastic to lower edge.

PADDED SASH

Stitch the side seam of sash and turn right side out. Insert padding and center it. Topstitch several lines through all layers. Tie at back.

TREAT BAG

Pattern, page 71.

Iron paper-backed fusible web to the wrong side of fabric scraps. Cut out images of a magic lamp and genie. Peel off the paper and iron the images onto the bag.

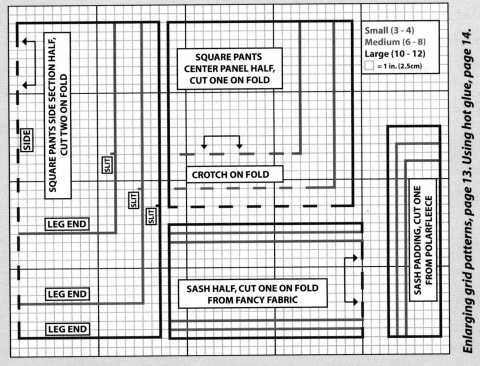

SQUARE PANTS SIDE SECTION HALF, CUT TWO ON FOLD

SIDE

SLIT

SLIT

SLIT

LEG END

LEG END

LEG END

SQUARE PANTS CENTER PANEL HALF, CUT ONE ON FOLD

CROTCH ON FOLD

SASH HALF, CUT ONE ON FOLD FROM FANCY FABRIC

SASH PADDING, CUT ONE FROM POLARFLEECE

Small (3 - 4)
Medium (6 - 8)
Large (10 - 12)
☐ = 1 in. (2.5cm)

Enlarging grid patterns, page 13. Using hot glue, page 14.

Damsel, Fairy & Baby Fairy

Damsels in their cone-shaped hats and elegant robes are medieval maidens of noble birth living in ancient castles. The beautiful, mythical fairy uses magical powers to help people.

damsel costume

CONE HAT

Stitch side seam of hat and interfacing separately. Turn the hat right side out and slip over interfacing. Topstitch the rims together. Decorate with stars and ribbons, all hotglued. Hotglue a scarf or a piece of fabric to back edge for a veil. For a chinstrap, cut a tiny hole at each side near lower edge, push elastic through holes, and knot securely.

UNDERGOWN & OVERDRESS
Pattern, 127.

Tie gold cords around mid-arms and waist as shown.

TREAT BAG FOR DAMSEL
Pattern, page 65.

WHAT YOU NEED

Size (approximate age in years)→	Small (3-4)	Medium (6-8)	Large (10-12)
Fairy and Damsel: Taffeta for undergown, 55" (140cm) wide:	1¾ yds. (1.60m)	2½ yds. (2.30m)	3½ yds. (3.10m)
Organza for overdress, 55" (140cm) wide:	1¾ yds. (1.60m)	2½ yds. (2.30m)	3½ yds. (3.10m)
Fairy: Organza for wings, 55" (140cm) wide:	1 yd. (1.00m)	1 yd. (1.00m)	1 yd. (1.00m)

Other supplies (for both Damsel and Fairy):
- ❑ elastic for neck opening
- ❑ fusible web for hem
- ❑ gold cord for sleeves and waist
- ❑ sewing machine
- ❑ needle and thread
- ❑ hot glue gun and glue sticks

For treat bag:
- ❑ fancy fabric
- ❑ lining fabric
- ❑ piece of narrow elastic
- ❑ cord for a drawstring

Additional supplies for Damsel:

For cone hat and veil:
- ❑ stiff, non-fusible interfacing
- ❑ leftover taffeta and organza
- ❑ fancy fabric scraps
- ❑ decorative ribbons
- ❑ scarf or fabric for veil
- ❑ elastic for a chinstrap

Additional supplies for Fairy:

For magic wand and pendant:
- ❑ wooden rod
- ❑ decorative ribbons
- ❑ stiff cardboard
- ❑ fake gems
- ❑ fancy fabric scraps
- ❑ cord

For wings:
- ❑ fusible web, 1 yd. of 26" wide or 1.00m of 66cm wide
- ❑ 2 yds. (1.80m) of 16-gauge galvanized wire
- ❑ wire cutters
- ❑ 2 yds. (1.80m) of decorative ribbon
- ❑ ½ yd. (0.50m) of wide twill tape
- ❑ four safety pins

For headband:
- ❑ gold knit fabric
- ❑ polyester fiberfill
- ❑ decorative ribbon
- ❑ fake flowers

Baby Fairy:
- ❑ fabric for hat, neck ruffle, and trim
- ❑ interfacing for hat
- ❑ narrow elastic for neck edge and chinstrap
- ❑ fusible web strip to hem the neck ruffle
- ❑ iridescent gift tissue or organza for wings and veil
- ❑ 16-gauge galvanized wire and wire cutters for wings
- ❑ adhesive tape
- ❑ double-sided foam tape
- ❑ sewing machine
- ❑ needle and thread

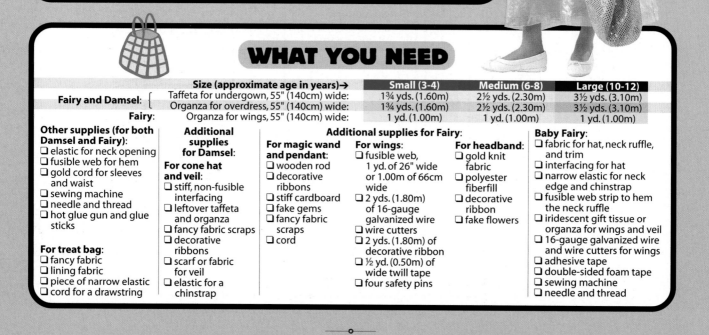

fairy costume

WINGS

Bend wire to match the pattern. Cut two layers of organza and one layer of fusible web, each 1" (2.5cm) larger all around than wire frame. With wire frame and fusible web between the organza layers, cover with press cloth, and press with a hot iron to fuse. Trim and hotglue ribbon around edges. Cut the twill tape in half, crisscross at center back, and stitch or hotglue, leaving ends free. Pin the free ends to dress back.

UNDERGOWN & OVERDRESS
Pattern, page 127.

Tie gold cords around midarms as shown.

PENDANT AND MAGIC WAND

Hotglue fabric to cardboard. Cut out three stars and decorate with fabric scraps, ribbons, and gems. Attach a long cord to one star for a pendant. Glue a rod end between two stars for a magic wand.

HEADBAND

Wrap fabric around fiberfill to make a soft headband and hotglue closed. Decorate with ribbons and flowers.

TREAT BAG FOR FAIRY
Pattern, page 65.

baby fairy costume

CONE HAT

Line hat with interfacing. Stitch side seam and turn right side out. Trim with ribbon or ruffle. Attach elastic for a chin strap. On right side, use double-sided foam tape to attach gift tissue to hat back seam for a veil.

NECK RUFFLE

Cut a rectangle, 12" x 45" (30cm x 115cm). Stitch short ends together. Fuse hem under. Stitch upper edge under into a casing and insert elastic.

WINGS

Twist wire to match the wing pattern. Wrap gift tissue around the wings and tape in place around center. Use double-sided foam tape to attach the wings to neck ruffle at back.

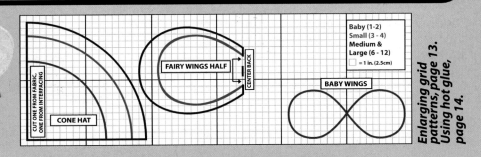

CUT ONE FROM FABRIC, ONE FROM INTERFACING

CONE HAT

FAIRY WINGS HALF

CENTER BACK

BABY WINGS

Baby (1-2)
Small (3 - 4)
Medium &
Large (6 - 12)
☐ = 1 in. (2.5cm)

Enlarging grid patterns, page 13. Using hot glue, page 14.

Little Red Riding Hood

Little Red Riding Hood is a fairy tale about a young girl sent to visit her ailing grandmother. With nothing but her hooded red cloak to shield her from the dangers of the forest, she outsmarts a crafty wolf and escapes his evil clutches.

CAPE

Stitch center back and hood seams. Cut long strips from leftover fabric for ties and stitch to front edge under chin.

PULL-ON VEST

Stitch shoulders. Stitch the right side seam. On right side, front only, stitch narrow vertical pleats (shown by dotted lines). Cut small holes under pleats, weave a cord through, crisscrossing, and tie at bottom. Sew a piece of Velcro to attach the left side seam.

DICKEY
from white Polarfleece.

Machine-baste one edge of long lace, gathering as needed. Sew several rows to front. Wear dickey under vest.

NO-PATTERN SKIRT

Measure and cut fabric in desired length to fit loosely around the child. Stitch center back seam. Fit a piece of elastic around waist and stitch ends together for a waistband. Gather waist edge of fabric and zigzag the elastic waistband to skirt.

 NO-SEW SHORTCUT

Make only the cape. Hotglue the seams.

TREAT CONTAINER

Line a basket with fabric.

SAFETY TIP

For a small child, cut the skirt short enough to prevent tripping.

Size (approximate age in years)→	Small (3-4)	Medium (6-8)	Large (10-12)
Red Polarfleece for cape, 60" (150cm) wide:	1⅜ yds. (1.30m)	1¾ yds. (1.60m)	2 yds. (1.80m)
Black Polarfleece for vest, 60" (150cm) wide:	⅜ yd. (0.40m)	½ yd. (0.50m)	⅝ yd. (0.60m)
White Polarfleece for dickey, 60" 150cm) wide:	¼ yd. (0.25m)	⅜ yd. (0.40m)	⅜ yd. (0.40m)

Other supplies:
- ❏ red Polarfleece, one length of skirt
- ❏ red cord for vest
- ❏ wide elastic for skirt waist
- ❏ white lace for dickey
- ❏ small piece of Velcro for vest closure
- ❏ a basket for treats & fabric for lining the basket

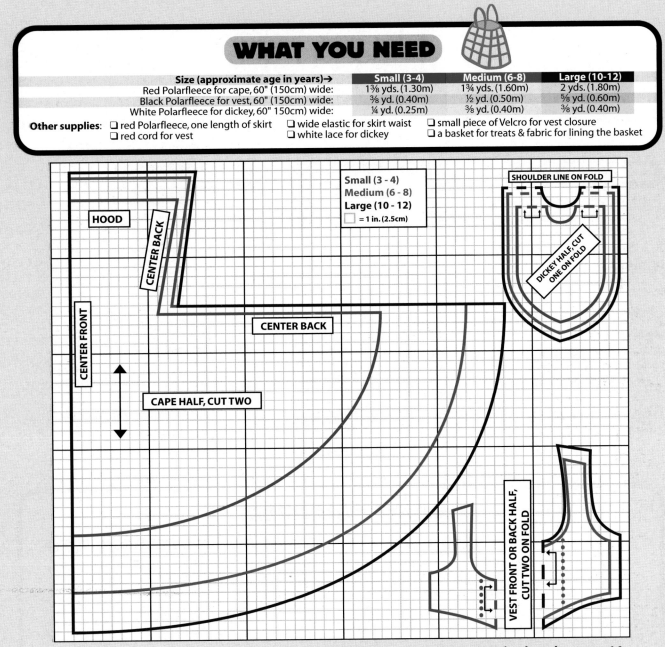

Small (3 - 4)
Medium (6 - 8)
Large (10 - 12)
☐ = 1 in. (2.5cm)

HOOD

CENTER BACK

CENTER FRONT

CENTER BACK

CAPE HALF, CUT TWO

SHOULDER LINE ON FOLD

DICKEY HALF, CUT ONE ON FOLD

VEST FRONT OR BACK HALF, CUT TWO ON FOLD

Enlarging grid patterns, page 13. Using hot glue, page 14.

Prince

Hero of ancient fairy tales, the handsome and brave prince lives in an old mountain-top castle. He has many dangerous and exciting adventures, slaying dragons and rescuing damsels in distress.

CROWN

Fuse metallic fabric to stiff interfacing. Cut out a crown, overlap ends, and hotglue closed. Decorate with gems or buttons, all hotglued.

CAPE

Stitch sides and center back. Hem front and lower edges. Gather neck edge slightly. Fold wide ribbon in half lengthwise and stitch around neck edge with ends extending to tie on front.

SHIRT
Pattern, page 17 (without lacy front panel).

Stitch bias binding around neck opening and sleeve ends to make casings and insert elastic.

VEST
Pattern, page 107.

SHIRRED SASH
See Dracula, page 17.

PANTS
Pattern, page 28.

Press waist edge under, stitch closed into a wide casing, and insert elastic. Hem leg ends. Press lower sides into sharp creases, fold backward, stitch in place, and trim with decorative cord, sewn or hotglued in place.

PENDANT

Hotglue fabric to cardboard and cut out a diamond-shaped piece. Decorate with fabric scraps, ribbons, and a fake gem, all hotglued. Make a hook from a paper clip and attach the pendant to a long cord.

WHAT YOU NEED

Size (approximate age in years)→	Small (3-4)	Medium (6-8)	Large (10-12)
Velvet, velveteen, velour, or similar fabric for cape, 45" (115cm) wide:	1⅛ yds. (1.10m)	1½ yds. (1.40m)	1¾ yds. (1.60m)
Fancy fabric for shirt, 45" (115cm) wide:	1½ yds. (1.40m)	2¼ yds. (2.10m)	2½ yds. (2.30m)
Taffeta or velvet for vest, 45" (115cm) wide:	½ yd. (0.50m)	⅝ yd. (0.60m)	¾ yd. (0.70m)
Lining for vest, 45" (115cm) wide:	½ yd. (0.50m)	⅝ yd. (0.60m)	¾ yd. (0.70m)
Taffeta or similar fabric for pants, 55" (140cm) wide:	⅞ yd. (0.80m)	1 yd. (1.00m)	1¼ yds. (1.20m)
Fancy fabric for sash, 55" (140cm) wide:	½ yd. (0.50m)	½ yd. (0.50m)	½ yd. (0.50m)

Other supplies:
- ❑ wide ribbon for cape neck edge, 40" (1.00m) long
- ❑ bias binding for shirt neck and sleeve ends
- ❑ narrow elastic for shirt neck and sleeve ends
- ❑ decorative cord for trimming pants
- ❑ wide elastic for waist   ❑ sewing machine
- ❑ hot glue gun and glue sticks   ❑ needle and thread

For crown:
- ❑ metallic gold fabric
- ❑ fusible web
- ❑ stiff interfacing
- ❑ fake gems or pretty buttons

For pendant:
- ❑ stiff cardboard
- ❑ fancy fabric scraps
- ❑ ribbons
- ❑ fake gem
- ❑ paper clip
- ❑ cord

For treat container:
- ❑ plastic pumpkin
- ❑ Polarfleece
- ❑ gold metallic fabric

Enlarging grid patterns, page 13.
Using hot glue, page 14.

SMART SHORTCUT

Make only the crown and cape. Wear an elegant shirt or vest, costume jewelry, and a long scarf around waist for a sash. Quick crown: Glue aluminum foil or gift wrap onto stiff cardboard, cut out a crown, and decorate as desired.

TREAT CONTAINER

Cover a plastic pumpkin first with Polarfleece and then with gold metallic fabric, hotgluing all.

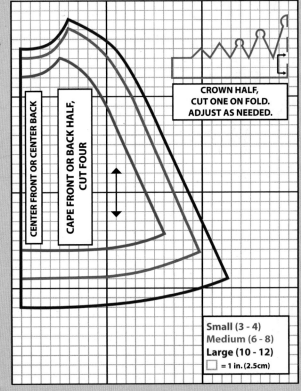

CROWN HALF,
CUT ONE ON FOLD.
ADJUST AS NEEDED.

CENTER FRONT OR CENTER BACK

CAPE FRONT OR BACK HALF,
CUT FOUR

Small (3 - 4)
Medium (6 - 8)
Large (10 - 12)
☐ = 1 in. (2.5cm)

Princess

A beautiful storybook princess wears gorgeous dresses and lives in an enchanted castle with high walls and towers, dreaming of her Prince Charming.

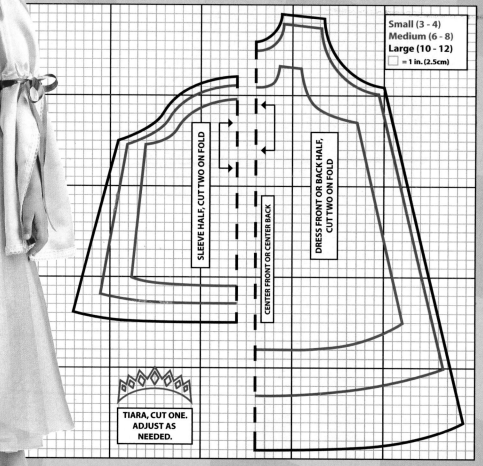

Small (3 - 4)
Medium (6 - 8)
Large (10 - 12)
☐ = 1 in. (2.5cm)

SLEEVE HALF, CUT TWO ON FOLD

CENTER FRONT OR CENTER BACK

DRESS FRONT OR BACK HALF, CUT TWO ON FOLD

TIARA, CUT ONE. ADJUST AS NEEDED.

Enlarging grid patterns, page 13. Using hot glue, page 14.

WHAT YOU NEED

Size (approximate age in years)→	Small (3-4)	Medium (6-8)	Large (10-12)
Fancy fabric (satin, taffeta, or similar) for dress, 55" (140cm) wide:	2 yds. (1.80m)	3¾ yds. (3.40m)	4¼ yds. (3.90m)
Organza or similar translucent fabric for overlay, 55" (140cm) wide:	1 yd. (1.00m)	1⅞ yds. (1.80m)	2¼ yds. (2.10m)

Other supplies:
- ❏ sewing machine
- ❏ a variety of wide and narrow decorative ribbons and lace for trimming the dress, sleeves, neck edge, and treat bag

- ❏ fusible web strip for hems
- ❏ needle and thread
- ❏ elastic for mid-arms, waist shirring, and overlay casing, ⅜" (10mm) wide, 2 yds. (1.80m)

For tiara:
- ❏ white crafting foam or cardboard
- ❏ white liquid glue ❏ gold glitter
- ❏ white plastic hairband
- ❏ hot glue gun and glue sticks

TIARA

Cut the tiara from white crafting foam or cardboard. Brush white glue on front and, while the glue is wet, sprinkle with gold glitter. Let dry. Hotglue the tiara to plastic hairband.

TREAT BAG
Pattern, page 107.

Make the bag from leftover fabric. Decorate with lace and ribbons.

DRESS

Stitch shoulder seams. Slit neck edge at center back for a comfortable fit. Trim slit edges with ribbon. Machine-baste sleeve tops and gather to fit armholes. Stitch sleeves to bodice. Stitch sides and underarms. Trim raw neck edge with ribbon, extending the ends to tie at back. On inside, stitch stretched elastic around the bust to shirr the fabric. Hem dress with fusible web. Slit sleeve ends up to elbows and trim raw edges with lace. On inside, stitch stretched elastic just above the elbows. On outside, tie ribbons on top of elastic into bows and handsew ribbon centers to underarm seams.

OVERLAY

Use the dress pattern. Measure and cut the fabric from underarms to the hemline. Cut one back piece on fold. Cut two front halves and round off corners of lower front. Stitch sides. Use fusible web to hem the front and lower edges. Stitch upper edge under into a casing and insert elastic to fit snugly under arms. On outside, sew loops to each side of overlay on top of elastic. Insert a long ribbon through loops, slip overlay on top of dress, and tie ribbon ends together on front.

Peter Pan

In the imaginary, joyous never-never land lives Peter Pan, the little boy who never grew up. Along with other lost boys, he spends his days fighting pirates and playing games.

HAT

Stitch side seams of both layers separately. Turn one hat right side out and pull over the other one. Topstitch rims together. Turn the brim up as shown and hotglue a feather in between. For a chinstrap, cut a tiny hole at each side near lower edge, push elastic through holes, and knot securely.

TUNIC

Stitch shoulder seams. Stitch sides. On inside, stitch stretched elastic around the waist.

WHAT YOU NEED

Size (approximate age in years)→	Small (3-4)	Medium (6-8)
Green Polarfleece for tunic, hat, spats, and treat bag, 60" (150cm) wide:	1¾ yds. (1.60m)	2¼ yds. (2.10m)
Green spandex for bodysuit and leggings, 60" (150cm) wide:	⅞ yd. (0.80m)	1⅛ yds. (1.10m)

Other supplies:
- ❑ metallic stars and gold glitter
- ❑ metallic cord for spats
- ❑ feather
- ❑ hot glue gun and glue sticks
- ❑ elastic for chinstrap, waist, and spats

SPATS

Adjust the size to fit over shoes. Stitch center front seam of each four separately. Stitch under-seam of curved front, sewing the triangular toe patch between edges at the same time. With wrong sides together, topstitch each two layers together along upper and lower edges. Stuff tips lightly with fabric scraps. For a strap under shoe, sew a piece of elastic to lower edge. Tie metallic cords around ankles, handsewing cord center to center back.

BODYSUIT
Pattern, page 45.

LEGGINGS

Use a stretch or a tight narrow zigzag stitch. Stitch inner leg seams. Turn one leg right side out and push it into the other leg. Stitch center seam. Stitch waist edge under into a casing and insert elastic. Hem leg ends.

 **FINAL TOUCH**

Trim the hat, tunic, spats, and bag. Drizzle hot glue to a small section at a time and immediately sprinkle with gold glitter and stars.

NO-SEW VERSION

Buy tights and bodysuit. Hotglue everything else.

 **TREAT BAG**
Pattern, page 71.

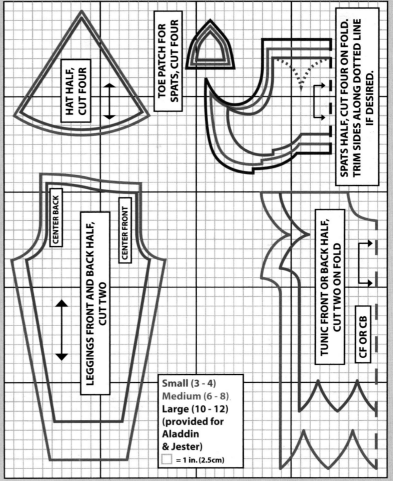

HAT HALF, CUT FOUR

TOE PATCH FOR SPATS, CUT FOUR

SPATS HALF, CUT FOUR ON FOLD. TRIM SIDES ALONG DOTTED LINE IF DESIRED.

CENTER BACK

CENTER FRONT

LEGGINGS FRONT AND BACK HALF, CUT TWO

TUNIC FRONT OR BACK HALF, CUT TWO ON FOLD

CF OR CB

Small (3 - 4)
Medium (6 - 8)
Large (10 - 12)
(provided for
Aladdin
& Jester)
☐ = 1 in. (2.5cm)

Enlarging grid patterns, page 13. Using hot glue, page 14.

Sprite

Diminutive, mischievous fairies, Sprites dance in meadows and forests. They bring good fortune and help to humans.

HEADBAND

Shape wire into a ring, overlap ends, and wrap with ribbon. Tie long ribbons around the ring. Hotglue silk flowers to the ribbons. Or make sweet pea flowers (see below).

SWEET PEA FLOWERS

Cut circles from gift tissue, 2-3" (5-8cm) wide, stacking layers to cut several at once. Cut elastic thread into pieces of about 6" (15cm) long. For each flower, fold a stack of three gift tissue circles in half, insert the elastic thread between center fold, and pull thread ends down while pushing folded paper edges tightly toward center. Tie ends and gently spread out the petals.

BODYSUIT

Use a stretch or a tight narrow zigzag stitch. Stitch shoulder seams. Stitch sleeves to bodice. Stitch sides, underarms, and crotch. Hem sleeve ends. Cut narrow strips from leftover spandex and stitch around leg holes and neck edge, stretching the strips slightly for a neat fit. Fold the strips under and topstitch in place.

LEGGINGS
Pattern, page 43.

SKIRT
See Hawaiian, page 113.

Trim waistband with ribbon. Cut paper ends into petals.

WHAT YOU NEED

Size (approximate age in years)→	Small (3-4)
Green spandex for bodysuit and leggings, 60" (150cm) wide:	⅞ yd. (0.80m)
Green Polarfleece for bolero, wings, and waistband, 60" (150cm) wide:	⅓ yd. (0.30m)

Other supplies:
- ❑ two packages of iridescent paper twist for wings and skirt
- ❑ 16-gauge galvanized wire for wings and headband
- ❑ wire cutters

- ❑ silk flowers for headband ribbons (or gift tissue and elastic thread to make flowers, shown)
- ❑ decorative ribbon for bolero and waistband
- ❑ elastic for waist   ❑ ribbons for headband
- ❑ hot glue gun and glue sticks

For treat bag:
- ❑ small piece of fancy fabric
- ❑ ribbon for a drawstring

BOLERO AND WINGS

Hotglue bolero shoulder seams. Trim bolero edges with ribbon. Bend wire into a figure 8 to match the wing pattern. Hotglue the wing frame to a rectangular piece of Polarfleece, slightly larger than the frame. Cut pieces of paper twist. Untwist and flatten each piece. Hotglue the pieces side by side onto wings, covering the wire and Polarfleece. Trim all around close to wire. Hotglue the wings to bolero back.

NO-SEW SHORTCUT

Buy bodysuit and tights or leggings. Hotglue everything else.

TREAT BAG

Pattern, page 65. (Adjust the size.)

To decorate the bag, cut leaf-shaped pieces from fabric. Hotglue stem ends around top edge of the bag. Add ribbon for a drawstring.

Enlarging grid patterns, page 13. Using hot glue, page 14.

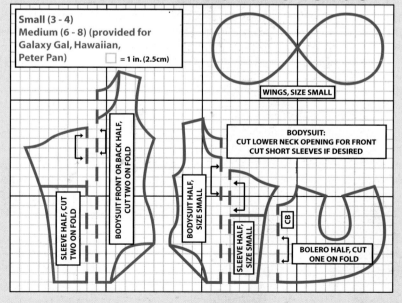

Small (3 - 4)
Medium (6 - 8) (provided for Galaxy Gal, Hawaiian, Peter Pan)
☐ = 1 in. (2.5cm)

WINGS, SIZE SMALL

BODYSUIT:
CUT LOWER NECK OPENING FOR FRONT
CUT SHORT SLEEVES IF DESIRED

SLEEVE HALF, CUT TWO ON FOLD

BODYSUIT FRONT OR BACK HALF, CUT TWO ON FOLD

BODYSUIT HALF, SIZE SMALL

SLEEVE HALF, SIZE SMALL

CB

BOLERO HALF, CUT ONE ON FOLD

Leprechaun

I n Irish folklore, the Leprechaun is a tiny old man who lives in remote places. He has a hidden pot of gold at the end of a rainbow. If you catch him, he might reveal its hiding place. But beware because he may trick you and vanish if you glance away.

TOP HAT
Pattern, page 61.

Hotglue wide elastic around crown for a band. Cut a mock buckle from white felt, a lucky four-leaf clover from green fabric, and hotglue in place. For a chinstrap, cut a tiny hole at each side near lower edge of crown, push elastic through holes, and knot securely.

TOP AND PANTS
Pattern, page 21.

Enlarging grid patterns, page 13.
Using hot glue, page 14.

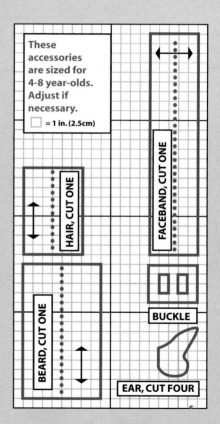

These accessories are sized for 4-8 year-olds. Adjust if necessary.

☐ = 1 in. (2.5cm)

FACEBAND, CUT ONE

HAIR, CUT ONE

BEARD, CUT ONE

BUCKLE

EAR, CUT FOUR

Size (approximate age in years)→	Small (3-4)	Medium(6-8)	Large (10-12)
Green Polarfleece for top hat, top, and pants, 60" (150cm) wide:	2 yds. (1.80m)	2⅝ yds. (2.40m)	3 yds. (2.70m)
Gray Polarfleece for beard and hair, 60" (150cm) wide:	½ yd. (0.50m)	½ yd. (0.50m)	½ yd. (0.50m)

Other supplies:
- ❏ stiff, non-fusible interfacing for hat, ⅔ yd. of 24" wide (0.60m of 60cm wide)
- ❏ small piece of brown fabric for ears
- ❏ wide black elastic for hatband, waist, belt, and boot-bands, 3 yds. (2.70m)
- ❏ narrow elastic for chinstrap and headstrap
- ❏ hot glue gun and glue sticks
- ❏ brown marker
- ❏ a small square of white felt for mock buckles
- ❏ sewing machine

For treat container:
- ❏ plastic pumpkin
- ❏ Polarfleece
- ❏ gold metallic fabric
- ❏ colorful fabric scraps

BEARD, HAIR, AND EARS

Fold the faceband in half lengthwise and hotglue ends together. Fold the beard in half lengthwise, hotgluing just the folded edge closed. Then cut the open edges into a fringe and pull into curls. Repeat for hair. Hotglue the beard and hair to the faceband. Cut the ears from brown fabric and hotglue double-layered, while stuffing lightly with fabric scraps. Hotglue the ears to the faceband sides and decorate with marker. For a headstrap, attach elastic behind ears.

BELT, BOOT-BANDS, AND BUCKLES

Cut a piece of wide black elastic for a belt and stitch ends together. Also cut two pieces for bands to slip over boots and stitch ends together. From white felt, cut mock buckles and hotglue to the belt and boot-bands.

TREAT CONTAINER

Cover a plastic pumpkin first with Polarfleece and then with metallic fabric, hotgluing all. Decorate with a rainbow and four-leaf clover, cut from fabric scraps and hotglued in place.

Gnome

Gnomes, especially popular and beloved in Scandinavia and other parts of Europe, are wise old dwarfs. Kind to nature and animals, they live underground and guard the precious treasures hidden in the earth. (Santa's Helpers, well-known in North America, are their cousins, and this costume can double for both roles.)

CONE HAT

Stitch side seam of each layer separately. Turn one hat right side out and pull it over the other. Topstitch the rims together. For a chinstrap, cut a tiny hole at each side near lower edge, push elastic through holes, and knot securely. To make a pompom, cut a 10" (25cm) square of Polarfleece. Cut two opposite edges into a narrow fringe along the stretchy cross-grain and pull to curl the ends. Roll the uncut center tightly and tie with a fabric strip. Hotglue or handsew to hat tip.

HAIR AND BEARD
from Polarfleece.

Cut one long edge into a fringe and pull into curls. Hotglue the uncut edge under hat rim for hair. Make beard to match hair. For a strap behind ears, attach elastic (see Cone Hat, above).

TOP AND PANTS

Pattern, page 21.

48

BELT AND BUCKLE
from Polarfleece.

Hotglue the belt in half lengthwise. Cut one buckle from Polarfleece and one from stiff cardboard or plastic. Hotglue them together and then hotglue the center bar to the belt end.

MITTENS
from Polarfleece.

Place child's hand on a piece of paper and draw all around, adding seam allowances and long wrists. (Or use the pattern as shown.) With right sides facing, stitch each two together. Slit seam allowance between thumb and forefinger and trim curves. Turn right side out. (No elastic is needed if wrists are long and narrow.)

TREAT CONTAINER

Cover a plastic cauldron and handle with red Polarfleece, hotgluing in place.

Enlarging grid patterns, page 13. Using hot glue, page 14.

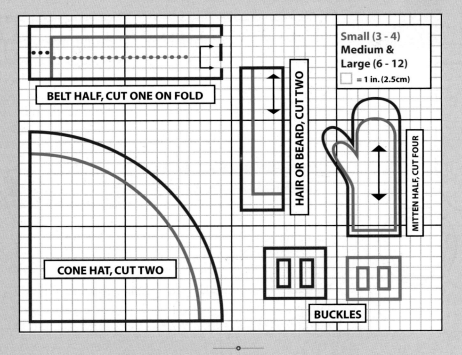

BELT HALF, CUT ONE ON FOLD

CONE HAT, CUT TWO

HAIR OR BEARD, CUT TWO

MITTEN HALF, CUT FOUR

BUCKLES

Small (3 - 4)
Medium &
Large (6 - 12)
❑ = 1 in. (2.5cm)

Gingerbread House & Gingerbread Man

Once upon a time there was an old woman who baked gingerbread cookies. One day while baking a gingerbread man, she opened the oven and the gingerbread man jumped out and ran away, shouting, "Run, run, as fast as you can, you can't catch me, I am the Gingerbread Man!"

In a classic folktale by the Grimm Brothers, two children, Hansel and Gretel, became lost in the woods. Very hungry and scared, they were happy to find a delicious gingerbread house covered with chocolate and candy. But it was a trap set by an evil witch who wanted to capture them. The clever children outsmarted the wicked witch and found their way safely home.

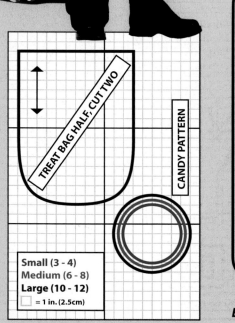

TREAT BAG HALF, CUT TWO

CANDY PATTERN

Small (3 - 4)
Medium (6 - 8)
Large (10 - 12)

☐ = 1 in. (2.5cm)

gingerbread house

BOX COSTUME

Remove top from box and turn upside down. Cut holes for arms and head. Make a roof from stiff cardboard and attach to box sides with duct tape.

DECORATE THE HOUSE

Cut white Polarfleece into icicle borders and icing corners as shown. Add other decorations as desired and hotglue all in place.

SPRAY-PAINT

Spray-paint the house brown. Spray-painting is best done outdoors. Protect the ground and your clothing. Let dry overnight.

TREAT BAG
Pattern, page 71.

Cut mock peppermint candies from white and red Polarfleece scraps and hotglue to the bag.

Enlarging grid patterns, page 13. Using hot glue, page 14.

WHAT YOU NEED

Size (approximate age in years)→	Small (3-4)	Medium (6-8)	Large (10-12)
Gingerbread man: Brown Polarfleece for top, pants, helmet, and mittens, 60" (150cm) wide:	2 yds. (1.80m)	3 yds. (2.70m)	3½ yds. (3.10m)
White Polarfleece for rickrack, 60" (150cm) wide:	½ yd. (0.50m)	½ yd. (0.50m)	½ yd. (0.50m)

For Gingerbread Man treat bag:
- ❑ white fabric
- ❑ cord for a drawstring
- ❑ brown and white leftover fabric scraps

Other supplies for Gingerbread Man:
- ❑ wide elastic for waist
- ❑ piece of foam or cardboard for headtop candy
- ❑ small square of red felt for decorations
- ❑ self-adhesive vinyl (with grid on paper side) to make rickrack pattern, ½ yd. of 17" wide (0.50m of 43cm wide)
- ❑ small piece of Velcro for helmet
- ❑ hot glue gun and glue sticks
- ❑ sewing machine

Supplies for Gingerbread House:
- ❑ large, lightweight box
- ❑ stiff cardboard for roof
- ❑ duct tape
- ❑ one can of nontoxic brown water-soluble spray paint
- ❑ white Polarfleece
- ❑ fabric scraps and crafting foam for decorations
- ❑ hot glue gun and glue sticks
- ❑ fabric for treat bag

gingerbread man

HELMET
Pattern, page 101.

Make a large mock peppermint candy from white Polarfleece hotglued over foam or cardboard. Trim with red Polarfleece and hotglue to helmet top.

TOP AND PANTS
Pattern, page 21 (or use an old sweatsuit).

Cut lots of large rickrack from white Polarfleece. Hotglue the rickrack to the costume as shown. Make candy buttons from fabric scraps and hotglue to front.

EASY RICKRACK FROM POLARFLEECE

Use the grid on backing paper of self-adhesive vinyl as a handy guide to draw a stick-on, symmetric, reusable pattern for large rickrack. Cut the pattern out. Peel off and discard the paper backing. Apply the vinyl pattern onto Polarfleece and cut along both edges. Pull the vinyl off the fabric and reapply to make more. Hotglue the prepared rickrack to the costume as shown.

TREAT BAG

Stitch sides and bottom. Stitch upper edge under into a casing and insert a cord for a drawstring. Cut a small gingerbread man from brown and white Polarfleece scraps and hotglue to the bag.

MITTENS
Pattern, page 49.

Pirate & Mini Pirate

Fearsome pirates ruled the seven seas, scanning the horizon for ships and robbing the treasures of merchant vessels. They stashed their booty in treasure chests and buried them in secret locations which could only be found using coded maps. Many of those old treasures have yet to be discovered.

HAT

Hotglue each of the two layers together around edges. Hotglue front to back at sides to fit around head, with loose ends extending. Cut out skull and crossbones from white Polarfleece or felt and hotglue to the hat.

VEST

Pattern, page 107.
Decorate as shown.

SHIRT
Use the top pattern, page 21.

Slit center front as shown. Trim neck and front slit with a facing cut from leftover fabric.

PANTS

Pattern, page 28.

Stitch leg ends into casings and insert narrow elastic.

HANDGUARD

Hotglue side seams. Push pirate hook through the hole at bottom.

BOOT-TOPS

Adjust size so shorter edge fits around boots. Hotglue each of the two layers together, overlapping back edges. Hotglue white fabric strips to lower edges. Slip over boots.

EYE-PATCH

Cut the patch from black Polarfleece and tie at back. (Sneaky shortcut: Use makeup to create a patch.)

BELT AND BUCKLE

Patterns, page 49.

Press the belt in half lengthwise, stitch or hotglue closed, and sew a piece of Velcro at back. Cut a large mock buckle from white Polarfleece and hotglue to front.

WHAT YOU NEED

Size (approximate age in years)→	Small (3-4)	Medium (6-8)	Large (10-12)
Red fabric for pants, 55" (140cm) wide:	⅞ yd. (0.80m)	1 yd. (1.00m)	1¼ yds. (1.20m)
Striped knit fabric for shirt, 55" (140cm) wide:	⅞ yd. (0.80m)	1¼ yds. (1.20m)	1½ yds. (1.40m)
Black fabric for vest, 45" wide:	½ yd. (0.50m)	⅝ yd. (0.60m)	¾ yd. (0.70m)
Fabric for vest lining, 45" wide:	½ yd. (0.50m)	⅝ yd. (0.60m)	¾ yd. (0.70m)
Black Polarfleece or felt for hat, belt, boot-tops, eye-patch, handguard, and treat bag, 60" (150cm) wide:	1 yd. (1.00m)	1¼ yds. (1.20m)	1½ yds. (1.40m)
White Polarfleece or felt for trimmings, 60" (150cm) wide:	⅛ yd. (0.10m)	⅛ yd. (0.10m)	⅛ yd. (0.10m)

Other supplies:
- ❏ wide elastic for waist
- ❏ narrow elastic for leg ends
- ❏ brown fabric or paper and black marker for treasure map
- ❏ plastic sword   ❏ plastic pirate hook
- ❏ hot glue gun and glue sticks

Mini Pirate:
- ❏ black Polarfleece or felt for hat and cape, ⅞ yd. of 60" wide (0.80m of 150cm wide)
- ❏ small scrap of white Polarfleece or felt
- ❏ lace
- ❏ hot glue gun and glue sticks   ❏ red button

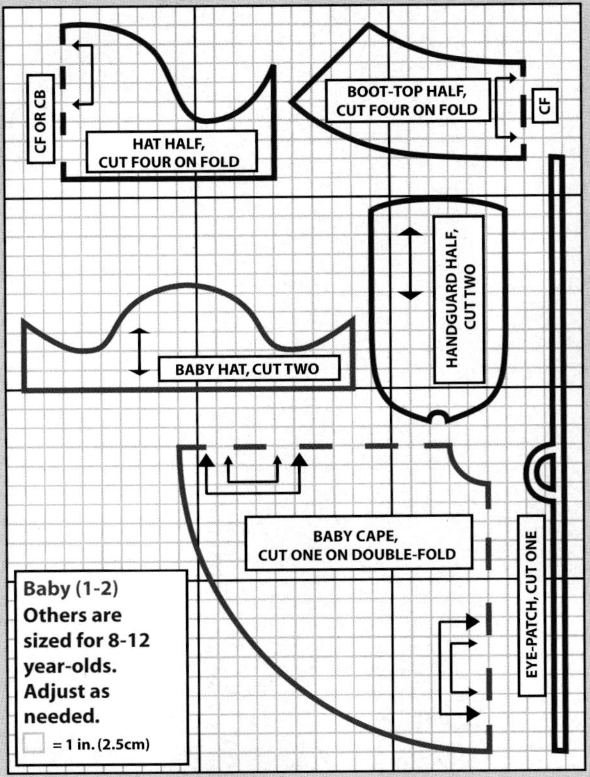

HAT HALF, CUT FOUR ON FOLD

CF OR CB

BOOT-TOP HALF, CUT FOUR ON FOLD

CF

HANDGUARD HALF, CUT TWO

BABY HAT, CUT TWO

BABY CAPE, CUT ONE ON DOUBLE-FOLD

EYE-PATCH, CUT ONE

Baby (1-2)
Others are sized for 8-12 year-olds. Adjust as needed.

☐ = 1 in. (2.5cm)

Enlarging grid patterns, page 13.
Using hot glue, page 14.

NO-SEW SHORTCUT

Wear a T-shirt and cutoff jeans. Cut the vest from black Polarfleece and hotglue shoulder seams. Or, cut sleeves off a castoff jacket for a quick vest. Wrap a scarf around head and knot at side.

TREAT BAG
Pattern, page 71.

Draw a treasure map on brown fabric or paper and hotglue to the bag.

HAT
See Pirate.

CAPE

Cut a large circle from black Polarfleece. Cut out a neck opening. Cut lower edge as shown. Decorate front with pleated lace and red button, all hotglued.

mini pirate

Swamp Monster

This mysterious creature, who lives in muddy swamps and seldom emerges from its habitat, is covered in decaying vegetation and creepy creatures.

BALACLAVA HELMET

Stitch or hotglue center front and center back seams.

DOUBLE-LAYERED BALACLAVA HELMET

This version is used for animal costumes on other pages.

Cut four pattern pieces. Stitch center front and center back seams of each of the two layers. With right sides together, stitch around face opening. Clip the seam and turn right side out. Topstitch lower edges together.

TRIM THE HELMET

Prop the helmet over a large can or bottle. Cut spikes from green crafting foam with points at top and slits at bottom. Spread the slits apart and hotglue to the helmet top. Hotglue trimmings all over as desired.

54

WHAT YOU NEED

Size (approximate age in years)→	Small (3-4)	Medium(6-8)	Large (10-12)
Green Polarfleece for helmet and treat bag, 60" (150cm) wide:	⅞ yd. (0.80m)	⅞ yd. (0.80m)	⅞ yd. (0.80m)

Other supplies:
- ❑ old dark sweatsuit
- ❑ trimmings from a dollar store, such as peat moss, Spanish moss, green bingo chips, green and silver glitter, plastic bugs and snakes, plastic feathery leaves and branches, green crafting foam, etc.
- ❑ green mini-gloves (one-size-fits-all)
- ❑ hot glue gun and glue sticks

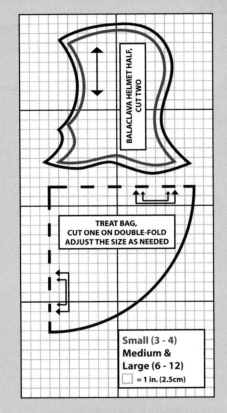

BALACLAVA HELMET HALF, CUT TWO

TREAT BAG, CUT ONE ON DOUBLE-FOLD ADJUST THE SIZE AS NEEDED

Small (3 - 4)
Medium & Large (6 - 12)
☐ = 1 in. (2.5cm)

Enlarging grid patterns, page 13.
Using hot glue, page 14.

TRIM THE COSTUME

Stuff an old dark sweatsuit with crumpled newspaper. Trim with creepy creatures to match the helmet, hotgluing all. Remove the newspaper.

GLOVES

Cut two creepy overlays with tapered points from green Polarfleece scraps. Hotglue to mini-gloves.

IF YOU PREFER SEWING

Instead of using an old sweatsuit, make top and pants from green Polarfleece, using patterns on page 21. Instead of using mini-gloves, sew a pair of easy Polarfleece gloves (see Astronaut, page 77).

TREAT BAG

Cut the bag from green Polarfleece. Cut the entire circular edge into a fringe. Cut holes all around below the bottom edge of fringe. Cut a long strip from Polarfleece and weave it through the holes for a drawstring.

Spy

During Halloween, a mysterious spy helps locate missing candy, coming to the rescue of little trick-or-treaters in distress and then disappearing wordlessly into the dark night.

WHAT YOU NEED

Size (approximate age in years)→	Small (3-4)	Medium(6-8)	Large (10-12)
Fabric for cape, 55" (140cm) wide:	1½ yds. (1.40m)	2¼ yds. (2.10m)	3¼ yds. (3.00m)
Polarfleece for mask and treat bag, 60" (150cm) wide:	⅔ yd. (0.60m)	⅔ yd. (0.60m)	⅔ yd. (0.60m)

Other supplies:
- ❑ small piece of Velcro for front closure
- ❑ hat from a thrift shop or flea market
- ❑ small piece of metallic self-adhesive vinyl for decorating the treat bag
- ❑ stiff, non-fusible interfacing for collar
- ❑ sewing machine

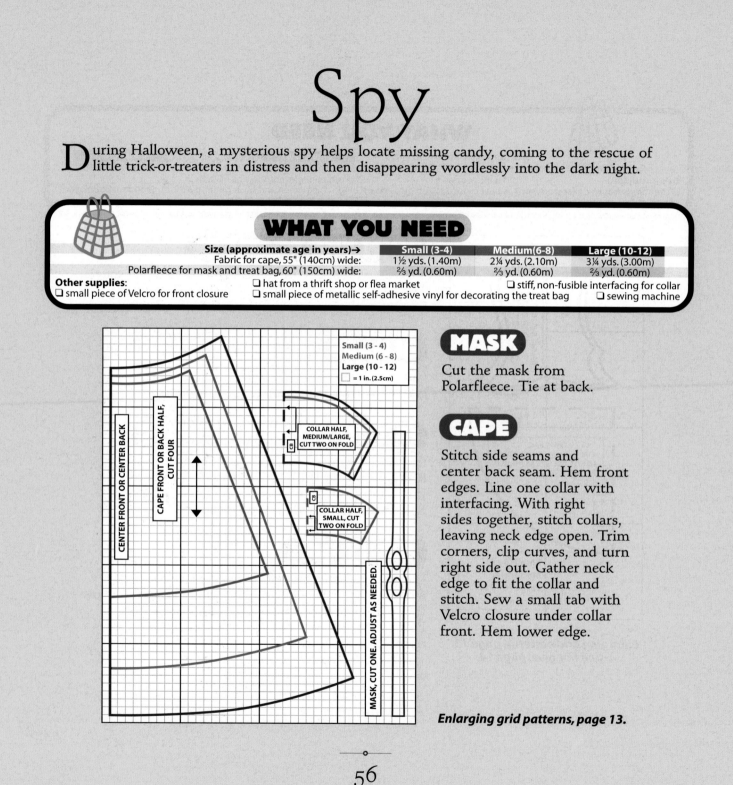

Small (3 - 4)
Medium (6 - 8)
Large (10 - 12)
❑ = 1 in. (2.5cm)

CENTER FRONT OR CENTER BACK

CAPE FRONT OR BACK HALF, CUT FOUR

COLLAR HALF, MEDIUM/LARGE, CUT TWO ON FOLD

COLLAR HALF, SMALL, CUT TWO ON FOLD

MASK, CUT ONE. ADJUST AS NEEDED.

MASK

Cut the mask from Polarfleece. Tie at back.

CAPE

Stitch side seams and center back seam. Hem front edges. Line one collar with interfacing. With right sides together, stitch collars, leaving neck edge open. Trim corners, clip curves, and turn right side out. Gather neck edge to fit the collar and stitch. Sew a small tab with Velcro closure under collar front. Hem lower edge.

Enlarging grid patterns, page 13.

SAFETY TIP

For a small child, cut the cape short enough to prevent tripping, and use makeup instead of mask.

TREAT BAG
Pattern, page 103.

Cut a large question mark from self-adhesive vinyl, peel off the paper, and apply the decoration onto the bag.

Jailbird

This jailbird is an outlaw on the lam. He finds trick-or-treating so irresistible that he can't help joining the merry celebrations while trying his best to avoid the long arm of the law.

CAP

Stitch the round edges together. Fold straight edge under and stitch in place.

TOP AND PANTS

Pattern, page 21. (Enlarge slightly for non-stretchy fabrics.)

Stitch shoulder seams of top. Slit neck edge of front as shown. Trim neck and front slit with a facing cut from leftover fabric. Stitch sleeves to bodice. Stitch sides and underarms. Hem lower edge and sleeve ends. Pin pants front to back. Stitch inner leg seams. Stitch center seam. Stitch side seams. Stitch waist edge under into a casing and insert elastic. Hem leg ends.

ID PATCHES

Cut two patches from white fusible interfacing. Fuse the patches onto the hat and top. Using a marker, draw mock stitching lines and convict's number on the patches. (Sneaky shortcut: Draw the numbers on stiff white paper and attach to the costume with double-sided foam tape.)

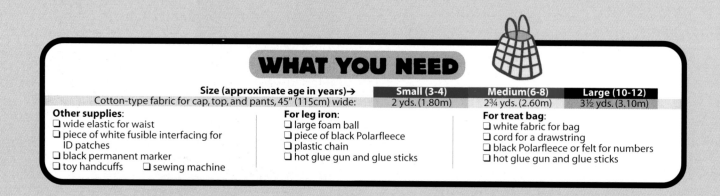

WHAT YOU NEED

Size (approximate age in years)→	Small (3-4)	Medium(6-8)	Large (10-12)
Cotton-type fabric for cap, top, and pants, 45" (115cm) wide:	2 yds. (1.80m)	2¾ yds. (2.60m)	3½ yds. (3.10m)

Other supplies:
- ❏ wide elastic for waist
- ❏ piece of white fusible interfacing for ID patches
- ❏ black permanent marker
- ❏ toy handcuffs   ❏ sewing machine

For leg iron:
- ❏ large foam ball
- ❏ piece of black Polarfleece
- ❏ plastic chain
- ❏ hot glue gun and glue sticks

For treat bag:
- ❏ white fabric for bag
- ❏ cord for a drawstring
- ❏ black Polarfleece or felt for numbers
- ❏ hot glue gun and glue sticks

LEG IRON

Hotglue pieces of black Polarfleece to cover a large foam ball. Cut a hole in the ball and hotglue one end of plastic chain in the hole.

SAFETY TIP
(Not shown in photo.)

To go trick-or-treating, tie the chain around one ankle. Fasten the chain to leg with duct tape to avoid dragging the ball on the ground.

TREAT BAG

Stitch sides and bottom. Stitch upper edge under into a casing and insert a cord for a drawstring. Cut large numbers from black fabric and hotglue to the bag.
(Sneaky shortcut: Use self-adhesive vinyl for numbers.)

Enlarging grid patterns, page 13.
Using hot glue, page 14.

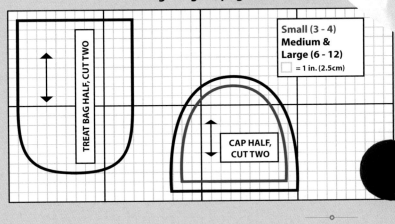

TREAT BAG HALF, CUT TWO

CAP HALF, CUT TWO

Small (3 - 4)
Medium & Large (6 - 12)
☐ = 1 in. (2.5cm)

Snowman

Whenever soft snow falls, you can be sure to find children brimming with anticipation, eager to rush outdoors to play. Before too long, there are snowmen wherever you look, happily created by little hands. Each snowman, though made according to the same simple method, is as different as the very snowflakes that were used to build it.

TOP HAT

Hotglue interfacing to crown around edges. Overlap short ends and hotglue into a tube. With interfacing in between, hotglue the brim layers together around outer edge. Slit inner edge of brim into small tabs, bend the tabs upward, and hotglue to the crown on the outside edge. Cut a long strip from white Polarfleece and tie on as shown, covering the tabs. For a chinstrap, cut a tiny hole at each side near lower edge of crown, push elastic through holes, and knot securely.

TABARD

Hotglue the shoulder seams. With wrong sides together, hotglue front to back along the right side seam. Sew pieces of Velcro or ties to attach the left side seam. From white Polarfleece, cut two snowman shapes, and hotglue to the tabard front and back around edges only. On inside, cut a small slit in the black tabard at chest level of front and back. Push a few handfuls of fiberfill through the slits.

60

BUTTONS

Hotglue three layers of black Polarfleece scraps together. With scissors, sculpt four irregularly-shaped mock coal chunks. Hotglue the chunks to the tabard front for buttons.

SCARF

Cut a scarf from Polarfleece. Cut ends into fringe. Cut stripes, rickrack, and diamonds from colorful fabric scraps and hotglue to scarf.

 ## TREAT BAG
Pattern, page 71.

From colorful felt scraps, create a snowman and other details as desired. Hotglue to the bag.

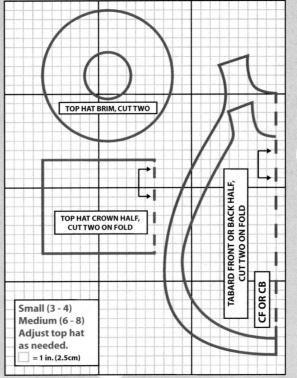

TOP HAT BRIM, CUT TWO

TOP HAT CROWN HALF, CUT TWO ON FOLD

TABARD FRONT OR BACK HALF, CUT TWO ON FOLD

CF OR CB

Small (3 - 4)
Medium (6 - 8)
Adjust top hat as needed.
☐ = 1 in. (2.5cm)

Enlarging grid patterns, page 13.
Using hot glue, page 14.

Monk & Nun

As members of religious congregations, monks and nuns live in monasteries and convents. They wear simple clothing and avoid worldly influences. Monks of medieval times lived in seclusion, transcribing scrolls to produce the first Bibles. Today, they are renowned for their cheeses, wines, and gardening. Nuns were the first teachers and nurses. In present day, they often assist with many different kinds of community work.

monk

LONG ROBE
Pattern, page 19 (without hood).

Tie a long cord around waist.

CROSS PENDANT

Hotglue brown Polarfleece to stiff cardboard. Cut out a large cross and wrap with decorative ribbon, hotgluing all. Add a hook made from a paper clip and attach the cross to a long gold cord.

HOODED SHOULDER CLOAK

Cut lower edge of cloak as shown. With folded edge at center top, stitch the slanted center back seam of hood. Stitch the hood to the cloak around neck opening, overlapping slightly at center front.

TREAT BAG
Pattern, page 103.

NO-SEW VERSION FOR BOTH: HOTGLUE THE SEAMS.

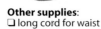

WHAT YOU NEED (MONK)

Size (approximate age in years)→	Small (3-4)	Medium (6-8)	Large (10-12)
Brown Polarfleece for hooded cloak, long robe, and treat bag, 60" (150cm) wide:	2¾ yds. (2.60m)	4¼ yds. (3.90m)	4½ yds. (4.10m)

Other supplies:
❑ long cord for waist

For pendant:
❑ paper clip
❑ gold cord

❑ stiff cardboard
❑ decorative ribbon
❑ hot glue gun and glue sticks

WHAT YOU NEED (NUN)

Size (approximate age in years)→	Small (3-4)	Medium (6-8)	Large (10-12)
Black Polarfleece for headscarf and long robe, 60" (150cm) wide:	1⅞ yds. (1.70m)	2⅜ yds. (2.20m)	2¾ yds. (2.60m)
White Polarfleece for headband and shoulder cloak, 60" (150cm) wide:	⅔ yd. (0.60m)	⅞ yd. (0.80m)	⅞ yd. (0.80m)

Other supplies:
❏ long cord for waist

For pendant:
❏ stiff cardboard
❏ gold cord
❏ decorative ribbon
❏ hot glue gun and glue sticks
❏ paper clip

For treat bag:
❏ white cotton fabric
❏ drawstring cord

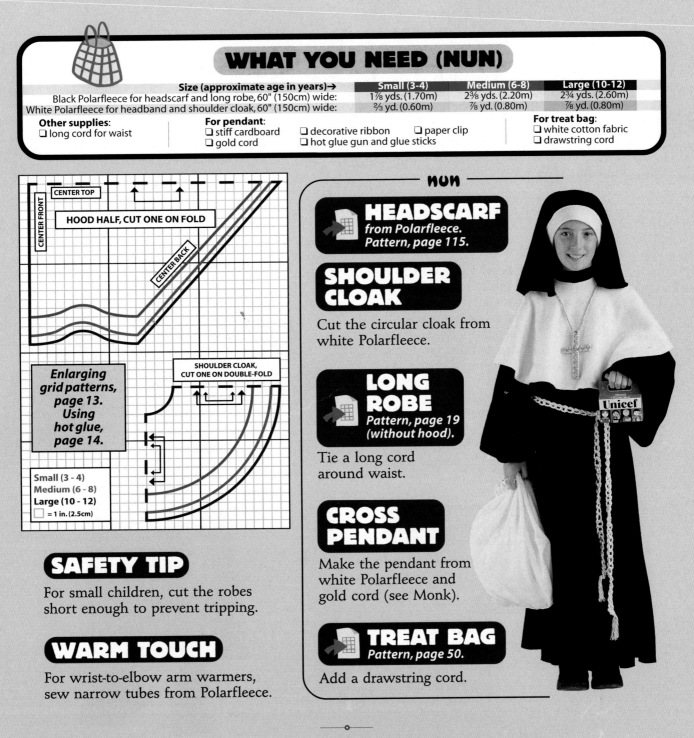

CENTER FRONT

CENTER TOP

HOOD HALF, CUT ONE ON FOLD

CENTER BACK

Enlarging grid patterns, page 13. Using hot glue, page 14.

SHOULDER CLOAK, CUT ONE ON DOUBLE-FOLD

Small (3 - 4)
Medium (6 - 8)
Large (10 - 12)
☐ = 1 in. (2.5cm)

NUN

HEADSCARF
from Polarfleece. Pattern, page 115.

SHOULDER CLOAK
Cut the circular cloak from white Polarfleece.

LONG ROBE
Pattern, page 19 (without hood).

Tie a long cord around waist.

CROSS PENDANT
Make the pendant from white Polarfleece and gold cord (see Monk).

TREAT BAG
Pattern, page 50.

Add a drawstring cord.

SAFETY TIP
For small children, cut the robes short enough to prevent tripping.

WARM TOUCH
For wrist-to-elbow arm warmers, sew narrow tubes from Polarfleece.

Shooting Star

H ave you ever gazed at the millions of luminous stars in the vast, dark skies? According to legend, if you make a wish when you catch a glimpse of a shooting star, your wish will come true.

STAR

Cut four star patterns from yellow Polarfleece for double-layered lining. Cut two star patterns from metallic fabric for a top layer. Hotglue each two Polarfleece layers together around edges. Hotglue the metallic fabric stars to Polarfleece stars around edges. With linings together, hotglue the completed stars front to back around three upper tips, leaving bottom open for neck. Cut face opening on front only. Stuff the three upper tips with fiberfill. Hotglue gold ribbons or long Christmas icicles under lower edge.

LONG ROBE
Pattern, page 19 (without hood).

Hotglue or stitch sides and underarms.

SAFETY TIP

For a small child, cut the robe short enough to prevent tripping.

WHAT YOU NEED

Size (approximate age in years)→	Small (3-4)	Medium (6-8)
Blue Polarfleece for robe, 60" (150cm) wide:	1⅞ yds. (1.80m)	2⅜ yds. (2.20m)
Yellow Polarfleece for lining of both star and treat bag, 60" (150cm) wide:	2 yds. (1.80m)	2 yds. (1.80m)
Metallic fabric for star top layer and treat bag, 45" (115cm) wide:	1½ yds. (1.40m)	1½ yds. (1.40m)

Other supplies:
❏ gold ribbons or long Christmas icicles for trimming the star
❏ polyester fiberfill to stuff star tips   ❏ hot glue gun and glue sticks

For treat bag:
❏ piece of narrow elastic
❏ cord for a drawstring

TREAT BAG

Adjust the size as desired. Cut one pattern piece from metallic fabric and one from Polarfleece. Treat the layers as one as you sew. Stitch side seam closed. On right side, stitch the top edges of fabric and lining together, press under, and fuse or hotglue in place. On inside, gather and knot the bottom tightly closed with a piece of elastic. Turn right side out. Cut small holes around upper edge and weave a cord through the holes for a drawstring.

Enlarging grid patterns, page 13. Using hot glue, page 14.

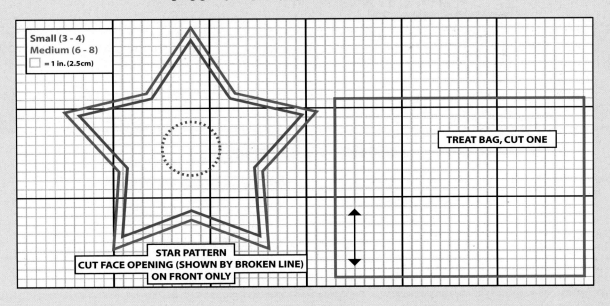

Small (3 - 4)
Medium (6 - 8)
☐ = 1 in. (2.5cm)

TREAT BAG, CUT ONE

STAR PATTERN
CUT FACE OPENING (SHOWN BY BROKEN LINE)
ON FRONT ONLY

Sun & Moon

In our universe, the earth and other planets revolve around the life-giving sun. Forever controlling the tides as well as our moods and the earth's cycles, the moon revolves quietly around the earth.

TABARD

Hotglue the shoulder seams. With wrong sides together, hotglue front to back along the right side seam. Sew pieces of Velcro or ties to attach the left side seam. Placing fusible web in between, iron blue metallic fabric to stiff interfacing. Cut it into two large circles for the sky. Iron paper-backed fusible web to the wrong side of metallic fabrics of several colors. Cut out a sun and a moon. From leftovers, cut details of your choice. Peel off the paper. Fuse the sun and the moon onto the large blue circles, trim edges, fuse on the details, and hotglue to the tabard front and back.

HEADBAND

Cut the headband from leftover metallic fabric. Handsew long sides together into a tube. Turn right side out and stuff with fiberfill. Sew ends together and wrap with ribbon as shown.

WHAT YOU NEED

Size (approximate age in years)→	Small (3-4)	Medium (6-8)
Black Polarfleece or felt for tabard, 60" (150cm) wide:	⅔ yd. (0.60m)	⅞ yd. (0.80m)
Stiff, non-fusible interfacing, 26" (66cm) wide:	1⅛ yds. (1.10m)	1⅓ yds. (1.20m)
Blue metallic fabric, 45" (115cm) wide:	⅝ yd. (0.60m)	1⅓ yds. (1.20m)
Fusible web, 26" (66cm) wide:	1⅓ yds. (1.20m)	1⅓ yds. (1.20m)

Other supplies:
❑ metallic fabrics (gold, silver, and bronze) for sun, moon, and details
❑ paper-backed fusible web, approximately 3-4 yds. (3.00m - 4.00m) depending on decorations and details
❑ hot glue gun and glue sticks

For headband:
❑ leftover metallic fabric
❑ needle and thread
❑ small amount of polyester fiberfill
❑ decorative ribbon

For treat container:
❑ plastic pumpkin
❑ Polarfleece
❑ metallic fabric

SMART SHORTCUT

Make the tabard as shown. Cut two large circles from blue posterboard for the sky. Cut the sun, moon, and details from foil gift wrap, and glue to the posterboard circles. Hotglue the posterboard circles to the tabard. The headband can be folded from gift wrap and decorated with ribbons.

TREAT CONTAINER

Cover a plastic pumpkin first with Polarfleece and then with metallic fabric, hotgluing all.

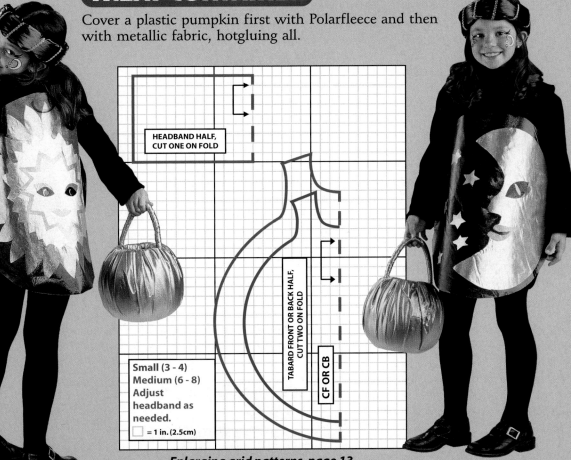

HEADBAND HALF,
CUT ONE ON FOLD

TABARD FRONT OR BACK HALF,
CUT TWO ON FOLD

CF OR CB

Small (3 - 4)
Medium (6 - 8)
Adjust
headband as
needed.

☐ = 1 in. (2.5cm)

Enlarging grid patterns, page 13.
Using hot glue, page 14.

Angel & Baby Angel

Watching over us, angels are celestial beings who protect us and help us in times of stress. People of many faiths throughout the world have belief in these ever-comforting guardian spirits.

angel

HALO

Form wire into a ring and wrap with decorative ribbon.

WINGS

Bend wire to match the pattern. Cut two layers from metallic fabric and one from fusible web, each about 1" (2.5cm) larger all around than the wire frame. With fusible web and wire frame between the two fabric layers, cover with press cloth, and press with a hot iron to fuse. Trim and cut side edges into scallops as shown. Cut two pieces of ribbon, 40" - 48" (1.00m - 1.20m) long each. Place ribbon ends crisscrossing on the underside of wings. Hotglue in place, leaving upper ends free and lower ends trailing for long ties. Use upper ends as tabs and pin to the dress. Tie lower ends into a large bow in front.

TREAT BAG

Stitch side seam. Pin lower edge to bottom circle and stitch. Fold top edge under about 4" (10cm) and stitch closed. Stitch close to first stitching line to make a casing. Cut a small hole in the casing and insert elastic, creating a ruffled top. Cut six pieces of ribbon, each 6" (15cm) long, and fold in half to make loops. On outside, stitch the loops to the bag on top of the elasticized casing. Cut a long piece of ribbon and insert it through the loops for a drawstring.

OVERDRESS AND UNDERGOWN
Pattern, page 127.

Tie long ribbons above elbows.

Size (approximate age in years)→	Small (3-4)	Medium (6-8)	Large (10-12)
Organza or similar fabric for overdress and bag, 55" (140cm) wide:	2½ yds. (2.30m)	3 yds. (2.70m)	4 yds. (3.60m)
White or off-white fabric for undergown and bag, 55" (140cm) wide:	2½ yds. (2.30m)	3 yds. (2.70m)	4 yds. (3.60m)
Metallic fabric for wings, 45" (115cm) wide:	⅞ yd. (0.80m)	1⅛ yds. (1.10m)	1¼ yds. (1.20m)
Fusible web for wings, 26" (66cm) wide:	⅞ yd. (0.80m)	1⅛ yds. (1.10m)	1¼ yds. (1.20m)

Other supplies:
- ❏ 16-gauge galvanized wire for halo and wings
- ❏ wire cutters
- ❏ decorative ribbon for halo
- ❏ wide gift ribbon with metallic edges, total needed for sleeves, wings, ties, and treat bag, approximately 7½ yds. (7.00m)
- ❏ narrow elastic for neck edge and treat bag
- ❏ sewing machine
- ❏ needle and thread
- ❏ hot glue gun and glue sticks
- ❏ two large safety pins

For Baby Angel:
- ❏ gold fabric, polyester fiberfill, and ribbon for halo
- ❏ 16-gauge galvanized wire and gold fabric for wings
- ❏ wire cutters
- ❏ white Polarfleece for cape, 30" x 30" (75cm x 75cm)
- ❏ metallic self-adhesive vinyl for star decorations
- ❏ hot glue gun and glue sticks

baby angel

HALO

Roll up a piece of gold fabric around fiberfill for a soft halo. Hotglue ends together and wrap with ribbon.

CAPE

Cut a large circle from white Polarfleece. Cut out a neck opening. Cut lower edge into scallops. Cut out stars from metallic self-adhesive vinyl, peel off the paper, and apply on the cape.

WINGS

Twist wire into tiny wings, wrap with gold fabric, and hotglue to the cape back.

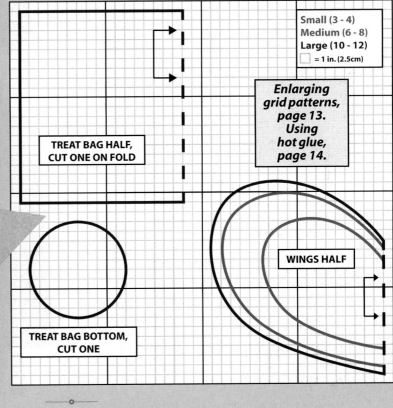

Small (3 - 4)
Medium (6 - 8)
Large (10 - 12)
☐ = 1 in. (2.5cm)

TREAT BAG HALF, CUT ONE ON FOLD

Enlarging grid patterns, page 13. Using hot glue, page 14.

WINGS HALF

TREAT BAG BOTTOM, CUT ONE

Christmas Tree

The modern Christmas tree originated in Germany, where an evergreen "paradise tree" was used as a prop in a medieval play. A wooden Christmas pyramid, topped with a star, had shelves to hold figurines. Eventually it merged with the paradise tree and the decorations included candles, candies, cookies, and paper chains. German settlers brought the custom to North America. Both indoor and outdoor Christmas trees have become popular symbols of yuletide festivities and peace on earth. Decorated with lights and beautiful ornaments, they are traditionally surrounded with gifts, a rite of kindness and goodwill.

TREE

Hotglue stiff wire between hems of the two front layers and then hotglue the side edges together. Repeat for the two back layers. With wrong sides together, hotglue front to back, leaving bottom open for legs and openings at sides for hands. Cut out face opening on front only.

> ***For medium size lining only***:
> *Piece fabric together as needed and hotglue, overlapping the seams.*

 FINAL TOUCH

Trim the tree with decorations, hotgluing all in place. Or let kids make their own decorations. Decorate the bag as shown with cord and little gift packages made from felt and ribbons, all hotglued in place.

70

WHAT YOU NEED

Size (approximate age in years)→	Small (3-4)	Medium (6-8)
Green Polarfleece for costume and treat bag, 60" (150cm) wide:	2⅜ yds. (2.20m)	4 yds. (3.60m)
16-gauge galvanized wire:	2 yds. (1.80m)	2⅝ yds. (2.40m)

Other supplies:
- ❏ dollar-store Christmas decorations (or supplies to make your own, such as crafting foam, pipe cleaners, gift ribbons, and felt)
- ❏ wire cutters
- ❏ hot glue gun and glue sticks

For treat bag:
- ❏ cord
- ❏ felt scraps
- ❏ ribbon

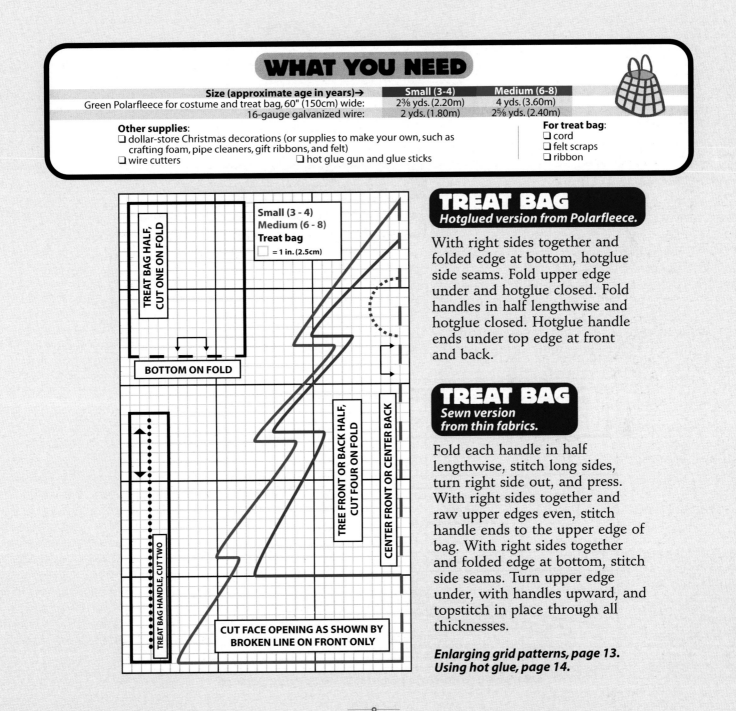

Small (3 - 4)
Medium (6 - 8)
Treat bag
☐ = 1 in. (2.5cm)

TREAT BAG HALF, CUT ONE ON FOLD

BOTTOM ON FOLD

TREAT BAG HANDLE, CUT TWO

TREE FRONT OR BACK HALF, CUT FOUR ON FOLD

CENTER FRONT OR CENTER BACK

CUT FACE OPENING AS SHOWN BY BROKEN LINE ON FRONT ONLY

TREAT BAG
Hotglued version from Polarfleece.

With right sides together and folded edge at bottom, hotglue side seams. Fold upper edge under and hotglue closed. Fold handles in half lengthwise and hotglue closed. Hotglue handle ends under top edge at front and back.

TREAT BAG
Sewn version from thin fabrics.

Fold each handle in half lengthwise, stitch long sides, turn right side out, and press. With right sides together and raw upper edges even, stitch handle ends to the upper edge of bag. With right sides together and folded edge at bottom, stitch side seams. Turn upper edge under, with handles upward, and topstitch in place through all thicknesses.

Enlarging grid patterns, page 13.
Using hot glue, page 14.

Galaxy Guy

Wondering about a possible life beyond our familiar planet, we earthlings fantasize about UFOs and aliens.

HELMET

Cover a toy helmet first with Polarfleece and then with metallic fabric, hotgluing all. Roll metallic silver fabric around fiberfill for a soft band and hotglue it around rim top. For an antenna, wrap wire around pen, pull out, add rolled-up ball of foil for a tip, and hotglue in place. Cut a piece of elastic for a chinstrap and hotglue ends under helmet edge.

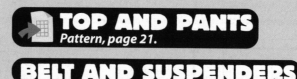 TOP AND PANTS
Pattern, page 21.

BELT AND SUSPENDERS

Cut top layer from metallic fabric and lining from Polarfleece. Stitch lining to fabric, each piece separately, leaving ends open. Turn right side out. Stitch Velcro closure at belt back. Hotglue suspender ends under belt at both front and back. Fold the crossbar in half, hotglue closed, and then hotglue ends under suspenders at midback.

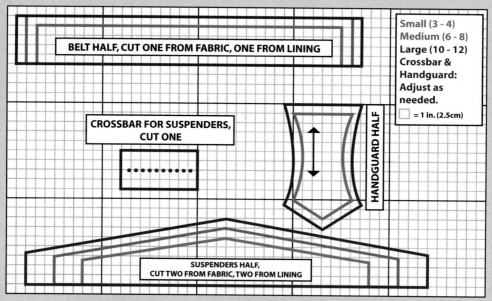

BELT HALF, CUT ONE FROM FABRIC, ONE FROM LINING

CROSSBAR FOR SUSPENDERS, CUT ONE

HANDGUARD HALF

Small (3 - 4)
Medium (6 - 8)
Large (10 - 12)
Crossbar & Handguard: Adjust as needed.

☐ = 1 in. (2.5cm)

SUSPENDERS HALF, CUT TWO FROM FABRIC, TWO FROM LINING

Enlarging grid patterns, page 13. Using hot glue, page 14.

HANDGUARDS

For each, cut two layers from Polarfleece and one from metallic fabric. With metallic fabric in between, stitch sides. Turn right side out. On inside, sew two loops from elastic to hook the handguard over thumb and middle finger.

 **SPATS**
Pattern, page 87.

Line top layer with interfacing. Stitch center front seam of each of the four layers. With right sides facing, stitch two layers together around upper edge. Turn right side out and topstitch around upper edge and lower edge. For a strap under shoe, sew a piece of elastic to lower edge.

FINAL TOUCH

Cut out simple lightning bolts from red fabric and hotglue to the costume as shown.

TREAT CONTAINER

Hotglue blue Polarfleece to cover a cardboard box. Trim with duct tape. Add a strap. Make an antenna to match the helmet. Hotglue all in place.

WHAT YOU NEED

Size (approximate age in years)→	Small (3-4)	Medium (6-8)	Large (10-12)
Blue Polarfleece for top, pants, handguards, spats, and treat container, and for the lining of both suspenders and belt, 60" (150cm) wide:	2½ yds. (2.30m)	3⅝ yds. (3.40m)	4¼ yds. (3.90m)
Stiff, non-fusible interfacing for spats, 26" (66cm) wide:	⅝ yd. (0.60m)	¾ yd. (0.70m)	⅞ yd. (0.80m)
Metallic silver fabric for suspenders, belt, and helmet band, 45" (115cm) wide:	⅝ yd. (0.60m)	¾ yd. (0.70m)	⅞ yd. (0.80m)
Blue metallic fabric for helmet and handguards, 45" (115cm) wide:	½ yd. (0.50m)	½ yd. (0.50m)	½ yd. (0.50m)

Other supplies:
❑ wide elastic for pants
❑ narrow elastic for spats and handguards
❑ piece of red Polarfleece or felt for decorations
❑ hot glue gun and glue sticks
❑ sewing machine

For helmet:
❑ plastic toy helmet
❑ polyester fiberfill
❑ stiff, flexible wire
❑ aluminum foil
❑ elastic for chinstrap

For treat container:
❑ cardboard box
❑ silver duct tape
❑ wire
❑ aluminum foil

Galaxy Gal

Science fiction deepens our curiosity about other beings. Do they exist, these aliens from outer space? Halloween is a perfect time to fantasize and create alien characters somewhat like us and yet different.

HEADBAND

Crinkle and then straighten a large sheet of foil. Roll it over polyester stuffing to make a fat headband. Hotglue closed.

BODYSUIT
Pattern, page 45.

LEGGINGS
Pattern, page 43.

WHAT YOU NEED

Size (approximate age in years)→	Medium (6-8)
Silver or gray spandex for bodysuit and leggings, 60" (150cm) wide:	1⅛ yds. (1.10m)
Quilted fabric for top, skirt, and boots, 45" (115cm) wide:	1½ yds. (1.40m)

Other supplies:
- ❑ small piece of Velcro for top closure
- ❑ metallic fabric scraps for armbands and decorations
- ❑ polyester fiberfill for armbands and headband
- ❑ small piece of fabric for cap-sleeve lining
- ❑ one package of narrow bias binding for top
- ❑ one package of wide bias binding for skirt
- ❑ fusible web and stiff interfacing for decorations
- ❑ aluminum foil for headband
- ❑ elastic for boot straps
- ❑ hot glue gun and glue sticks
- ❑ sewing machine   ❑ needle and thread

For treat container:
- ❑ plastic pumpkin
- ❑ Polarfleece
- ❑ metallic fabric

74

TOP

Stitch shoulder seams and side seams. Trim armholes and neck edge with bias binding. Hem lower edge. Stitch Velcro at back edges. Line cap sleeves, turn right side out, and stitch under shoulder edges.

SKIRT

Adjust for a snug fit. Stitch side seams. Stitch wide bias binding around hem and waist, turn under, and stitch closed.

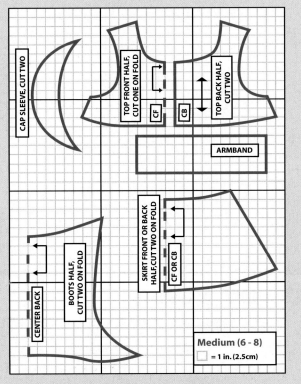

Enlarging grid patterns, page 13.
Using hot glue, page 14.

ARMBANDS

Stitch long edges together and turn right side out. Stuff with fiberfill and sew ends together.

BOOTS

(Add stiff interfacing and lining if the fabric is not stiff enough). Stitch front seam. Fold upper and lower edges under and topstitch in place. For a strap under shoe, sew a piece of elastic to lower edge.

FINAL TOUCH

Fuse metallic fabric to stiff interfacing. Cut out lightning bolts and other decorations for headband, top, and boots. Hotglue in place.

TREAT CONTAINER

Cover a plastic pumpkin first with Polarfleece and then with metallic fabric, hotgluing all.

Astronaut

Astronauts, highly trained for both the physical and psychological demands of a space mission, have advanced degrees in physics, chemistry, and other sciences. They pilot their spaceships and conduct scientific experiments during space flights. Much of their training takes place in both computer-controlled simulators and full-size spacecraft simulators.

 **COVERALLS**
Pattern, page 89.

Stitch ribknit bands around neck and sleeve ends. Make crests and flags from colorful felt and hotglue to the costume.

 **HELMET**

Cut the helmet from posterboard or corrugated cardboard. Crinkle and then straighten a large sheet of foil. Hotglue to cover the helmet. (Use Polarfleece scraps to protect your hands.) Overlap back edges and hotglue closed. Wrap wire around pen, pull out, add rolled-up ball of foil for a tip, and hotglue at helmet rim for an antenna.

 **OXYGEN TANK AND TUBE**

Cover a large cereal box and flexible tube with crinkled foil, hotgluing all. Cut the straps from Polarfleece, hotglue in half lengthwise and then to the oxygen tank, backpack-style. Cut a hole in one side of the box. Hotglue one end of the tube inside the hole and duct-tape the other end securely to the helmet.

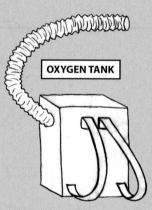

OXYGEN TANK

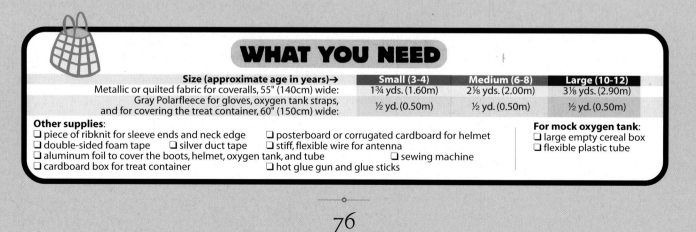

WHAT YOU NEED

Size (approximate age in years)→	Small (3-4)	Medium (6-8)	Large (10-12)
Metallic or quilted fabric for coveralls, 55" (140cm) wide:	1¾ yds. (1.60m)	2⅛ yds. (2.00m)	3⅛ yds. (2.90m)
Gray Polarfleece for gloves, oxygen tank straps, and for covering the treat container, 60" (150cm) wide:	½ yd. (0.50m)	½ yd. (0.50m)	½ yd. (0.50m)

Other supplies:
- ❏ piece of ribknit for sleeve ends and neck edge
- ❏ double-sided foam tape   ❏ silver duct tape
- ❏ aluminum foil to cover the boots, helmet, oxygen tank, and tube
- ❏ cardboard box for treat container
- ❏ posterboard or corrugated cardboard for helmet
- ❏ stiff, flexible wire for antenna
- ❏ sewing machine
- ❏ hot glue gun and glue sticks

For mock oxygen tank:
- ❏ large empty cereal box
- ❏ flexible plastic tube

GLOVES FROM POLARFLEECE

GLOVE HALF, CUT FOUR

Place child's hand on double-layered Polarfleece with fingers spread. Use a crayon to draw around fingers adding a long wrist. Draw a second line all around as you would for mittens. Cut out the mitten shapes but do not cut yet between the fingers. On right side, stitch the two layers together around fingers. Cut the stitching lines apart between fingers and trim close to the stitching lines. Repeat for the other hand.

BOOTS

Crinkle and then straighten a large sheet of aluminum foil. Cover any boots temporarily with the crinkled foil using duct tape and double-sided foam tape to secure loose edges.

TREAT CONTAINER

Hotglue Polarfleece around a cardboard box. Make a strap from Polarfleece and hotglue ends in place. Decorate as desired.

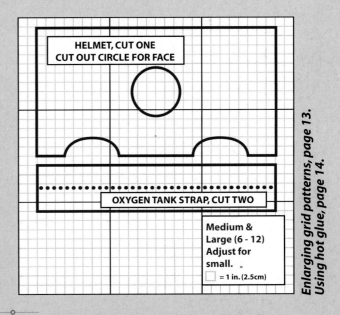

**HELMET, CUT ONE
CUT OUT CIRCLE FOR FACE**

OXYGEN TANK STRAP, CUT TWO

Medium & Large (6 - 12) Adjust for small.

☐ = 1 in. (2.5cm)

Enlarging grid patterns, page 13.
Using hot glue, page 14.

77

Octopus

Secretive and intelligent by nature, the octopus lives in crevices along the rocky bottom of tropical and temperate seas. If threatened, it can rapidly change its skin color and release an inky substance as a screen. Making a rare land appearance on Halloween night, the great octopus lends its image to children and protects them with eight powerful arms bearing suction cups with immense holding power.

HELMET

Stitch front and back seams, top layer and lining separately. With right sides facing, stitch the layers together around face opening. Turn right side out. Push fiberfill between the top layer and lining. Baste lower raw edges together.

ARMS

Stitch the top layers of arms together side by side at slanted shoulder seams to form a circle. Repeat for the lining. With right sides together, stitch top layer to lining around arm edges. Trim and clip corners. Turn right side out. Stitch the entire upper edge to helmet around neck opening.

🍒 FINAL TOUCH

Lightly stuff the three arms on front and the three at back with fiberfill and then hotglue the upper edges closed. Leave the other two unstuffed with upper edges open for child's arms and cut slits at bottom ends for child's hands. Cut large rings from purple Polarfleece and hotglue under arms for suction cups as shown.

TREAT BAG
Pattern, page 71.

Cut decorative images from fabric scraps and hotglue to the bag as shown.

Enlarging grid patterns, page 13. Using hot glue, page 14.

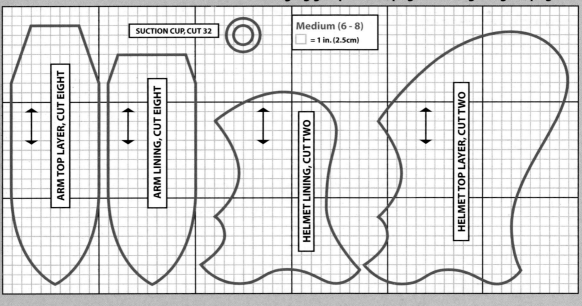

Bat

Bats emit high-frequency sounds, using the returning echoes to identify the direction and distance of prey and obstacles. Vampire bats, the eerie creatures of the night that survive only by sucking blood from their victims, are the inspiration behind the legend of Count Dracula. Existing for millions of years, vampire bats are found in the tropical and subtropical regions of Central and South America where they dwell in caves, mines, and tree hollows.

CAPE

Sew small pieces of Velcro for underarm closure. On inside, hotglue polyester boning or wire along shoulders to stiffen. Cover the wire with a strip of Polarfleece for comfort and hotglue in place. Cut stripes and a large moon from yellow Polarfleece, a bat from black Polarfleece, and hotglue to cape as shown.

HELMET
Pattern, page 101.

Hotglue two black forehead patches together and add yellow trim on top. Hotglue the patch to helmet front.

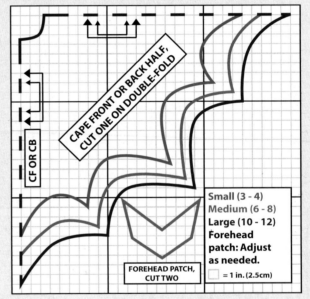

CF OR CB

CAPE FRONT OR BACK HALF, CUT ONE ON DOUBLE-FOLD

Small (3 - 4)
Medium (6 - 8)
Large (10 - 12)
Forehead patch: Adjust as needed.

☐ = 1 in. (2.5cm)

FOREHEAD PATCH, CUT TWO

Enlarging grid patterns, page 13.
Using hot glue, page 14.

WHAT YOU NEED

Size (approximate age in years)→	Small (3-4)	Medium (6-8)	Large (10-12)
Black Polarfleece or felt for cape, helmet, and treat bag, 60" (150cm) wide:	1¾ yds. (1.60m)	2 yds. (1.80m)	2¼ yds. (2.10m)
Yellow Polarfleece or felt for decorations, 60" (150cm) wide:	¼ yd. (0.25m)	¼ yd. (0.25m)	¼ yd. (0.25m)

Other supplies:
☐ Velcro, ½ yd. (0.50m)
☐ wire cutters
☐ polyester boning or 16-gauge galvanized wire, 1⅜ yds. (1.30m)
☐ hot glue gun and glue sticks

TREAT BAG
Pattern, page 71.

Decorate the bag to match the cape as shown.

NO-SEW VERSION

Make a balaclava helmet, page 55. Hotglue everything. Handsew snaps or pieces of Velcro for underarm closure.

Bumblebee

Bumblebees live in organized colonies and fly from blossom to blossom, cross-pollinating flowering plants. Before hibernating for the winter, the queen bee lends her warm costume so a small child can gather Halloween candies.

HELMET
Pattern, page 101.

Make two pompoms from yellow Polarfleece (see page 91). Cover stiff wire with a strip of black Polarfleece and hotglue the ends to pompoms. Bend the center in a U-shape. Hotglue the yellow forehead patch on top of the black one, with bent antenna wire centered in between, and hotglue to helmet front. Fold lower tab ends under and hotglue in place.

TABARD
Pattern, page 61.

Cut four pattern pieces from yellow Polarfleece. Hotglue the shoulder seams, each of the two layers separately. With wrong sides together, place the layers on top of each other and hotglue around all edges. Hotglue front to back along the right side seam. Sew pieces of Velcro or ties to attach the left side seam. Cut wide stripes from black Polarfleece and hotglue to the costume. On inside, cut a small slit, both front and back, at chest level of inner layer only. Push a few handfuls of fiberfill through the slits.

WHAT YOU NEED

Size (approximate age in years)→	Small (3-4)	Medium (6-8)
Yellow Polarfleece for tabard and helmet, 60" (150cm) wide:	2 yds. (1.80m)	2⅜ yds. (2.20m)
Black Polarfleece for stripes, 60" (150cm) wide:	½ yd. (0.50m)	½ yd. (0.50m)
White Polarfleece for wings, 60" (150cm) wide:	½ yd. (0.50m)	½ yd. (0.50m)

Other supplies:
- ❏ small piece of Velcro for helmet closure
- ❏ stiff floral wire or wire hanger for antennas
- ❏ wire cutters
- ❏ one bag of polyester fiberfill
- ❏ gold glitter for wings
- ❏ hot glue gun and glue sticks

For treat bag:
- ❏ fabric for bag
- ❏ fabric scraps and gold glitter for decoration

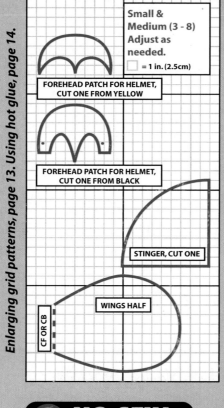

Enlarging grid patterns, page 13. Using hot glue, page 14.

Small & Medium (3 - 8) Adjust as needed.

☐ = 1 in. (2.5cm)

FOREHEAD PATCH FOR HELMET, CUT ONE FROM YELLOW

FOREHEAD PATCH FOR HELMET, CUT ONE FROM BLACK

STINGER, CUT ONE

WINGS HALF

CF OR CB

STINGER

Cut the stinger from yellow Polarfleece. Cut curved stripes from black Polarfleece and hotglue to stinger. Overlap the stinger edges and hotglue closed into a cone. Stuff with fiberfill and hotglue to tabard back bottom.

WINGS

Bend wire to match the wing pattern. Hotglue it to white Polarfleece. Trim, leaving 1/2" (12mm) of fabric all around the wire. Fold fabric edge over to cover the wire and hotglue in place. A small section at a time, drizzle hotglue onto wings and immediately sprinkle with gold glitter for veins. Hotglue the wings to the tabard back.

NO-SEW HELMET

Balaclava helmet, pattern on page 55.

Hotglue the seams.

TREAT BAG

Pattern, page 71.

Cut flower petals and a bee from fabric scraps and hotglue to the bag.

Ladybug & Baby Ladybug

"Ladybird, ladybird, fly away home..." This nursery rhyme has variations in many countries. When you find a ladybug, it is considered good luck. Just put the little beetle on your fingertip and gently blow on it so that it will fly away. These bugs are beneficial to your garden and the environment.

 **HELMET**
Pattern, page 101.

See Bumblebee, page 82, for antennas and forehead patch.

TABARD

Hotglue the shoulder seams, each of the two layers separately. With wrong sides together, hotglue the layers together around all edges. Hotglue front to back along the right side seam. Sew pieces of Velcro or ties to attach the left side seam.

 **FINAL TOUCH**

From black Polarfleece, cut yoke, center band, and ten large dots (as shown in the pattern), and hotglue to the costume front as shown. Repeat for back. On inside, cut a small slit, both front and back, at chest level of lining only. Push a few handfuls of fiberfill through the slits.

WHAT YOU NEED

Size (approximate age in years)→	Small (3-4)	Medium (6-8)
Ladybug: Red Polarfleece for tabard and treat bag, 60" (150cm) wide:	1¾ yds. (1.60m)	2⅛ yds. (2.00m)
Black Polarfleece for helmet and trimmings, 60" (150cm) wide:	¾ yd. (0.70m)	1 yd. (1.00m)

Other supplies:
- Velcro for helmet closure and tabard side
- stiff, flexible wire for antennas
- wire cutters
- one bag of polyester fiberfill
- hot glue gun and glue sticks

For Baby Ladybug:
- red Polarfleece, 1 yd. of 60" wide (1.00m of 150cm wide)
- black Polarfleece, ⅝ yd. of 60" wide (0.60m of 150cm wide)
- stiff, flexible wire for antennas
- wire cutters
- hot glue gun and glue sticks

NO-SEW HELMET

Balaclava helmet pattern, page 55.

Hotglue the seams.

TREAT BAG

Hotglue each of the two bag layers together around edges. Hotglue each pair of handles together. Hotglue handle ends under top edge at front and back. Hotglue front to back, leaving top edge open. Cut decorative details from black Polarfleece and hotglue to the bag as shown.

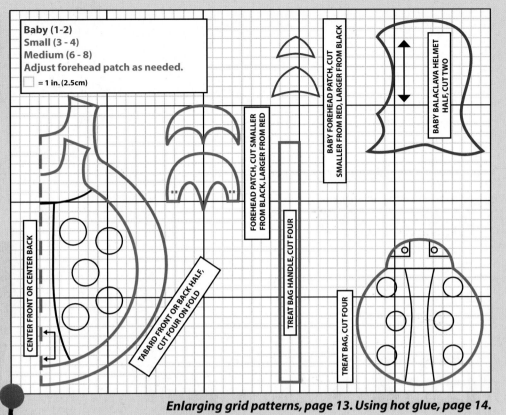

Baby (1-2)
Small (3 - 4)
Medium (6 - 8)
Adjust forehead patch as needed.

☐ = 1 in. (2.5cm)

FOREHEAD PATCH, CUT SMALLER FROM BLACK, LARGER FROM RED

BABY FOREHEAD PATCH, CUT SMALLER FROM RED, LARGER FROM BLACK

BABY BALACLAVA HELMET HALF, CUT TWO

CENTER FRONT OR CENTER BACK

TABARD FRONT OR BACK HALF, CUT FOUR ON FOLD

TREAT BAG HANDLE, CUT FOUR

TREAT BAG, CUT FOUR

Enlarging grid patterns, page 13. Using hot glue, page 14.

baby ladybug

CAPE

Cut a large circle from red Polarfleece. Cut out a neck opening. Cut stripes and dots from black Polarfleece and hotglue to the cape.

BALACLAVA HELMET

Hotglue center front and center back seams. Add antennas (see Ladybug). Hotglue antennas and the forehead patch to the helmet and add black dots as shown.

Mouse & Cheese

The common mouse is a scampering rodent that becomes a merciless predator on Halloween night in its quest to nibble on something delicious. There it is, an amazing treat almost within its reach, a great big chunk of fresh cheese.

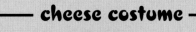

cheese costume

COSTUME
Adjust the size as needed.

Cut the pieces out of foam. With right sides facing out and using a long needle and strong thread, sew the pieces together into a wedge of cheese. Cut out a few holes for an authentic look.

SPRAY-PAINT

Spray-paint the costume yellow. Spray-painting is best done outdoors. Protect the ground and your clothing. Let dry overnight.

WHAT YOU NEED

	Size (approximate age in years)→	Small (3-4)	Medium (6-8)	Large (10-12)
Mouse:	Gray Polarfleece for coveralls, helmet, mittens, and spats, 60" (150cm) wide:	2½ yds. (2.30m)	3⅜ yds. (3.10m)	3⅝ yds. (3.40m)
	Contrasting Polarfleece for ears, mitten palms, and treat bag, 60" (150cm) wide:	⅓ yd. (0.30m)	⅓ yd. (0.30m)	⅓ yd. (0.30m)
	Black Polarfleece for tail, 60" (150cm) wide:	¼ yd. (0.25m)	¼ yd. (0.25m)	¼ yd. (0.25m)

Other supplies for Mouse:
- ❑ small piece of Velcro for helmet
- ❑ elastic for spats
- ❑ needle and thread
- ❑ long zipper for front
- ❑ sewing machine
- ❑ hot glue gun and glue sticks

For Cheese:
- ❑ foam sheeting of one inch (2.5 cm) thickness, one roll, 72" x 36" (1.80m x 90cm)
- ❑ long darning needle and strong thread
- ❑ one can of nontoxic yellow water-soluble spray paint
- ❑ fabric for treat bag

mouse costume

 **HELMET**
Pattern, page 101.

Stitch curved seams of ears, stuff with fabric scraps, and handsew to the helmet.

 **COVERALLS**
Pattern, page 89.

Roll up a long piece of Polarfleece into a tail, hotglue closed, and handsew to the costume.

 **MITTENS**
Pattern, page 49.

 SPATS

Adjust the size to fit over shoes. Stitch center front seam of each. With right sides facing, stitch each two layers together around upper edge. Turn right side out and topstitch close to upper edge, creating a casing. On inside, cut a small hole in the casing and insert elastic. Topstitch lower edges together. For a strap under shoe, sew a piece of elastic to lower edge.

SAFETY TIP

Make the tail short enough to prevent tripping.

 **TREAT BAG FOR EACH**
Pattern, page 71.

Sew or hotglue the seams and handle.

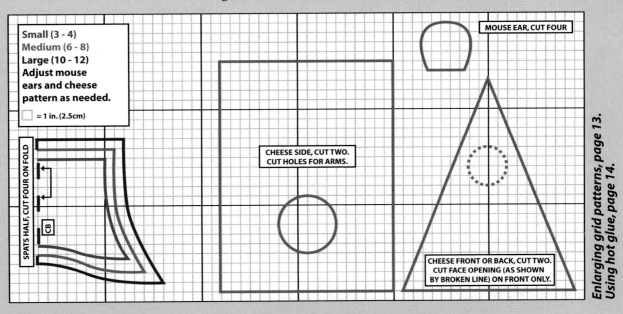

Small (3 - 4)
Medium (6 - 8)
Large (10 - 12)
Adjust mouse ears and cheese pattern as needed.

☐ = 1 in. (2.5cm)

SPATS HALF, CUT FOUR ON FOLD

CB

MOUSE EAR, CUT FOUR

CHEESE SIDE, CUT TWO.
CUT HOLES FOR ARMS.

CHEESE FRONT OR BACK, CUT TWO.
CUT FACE OPENING (AS SHOWN BY BROKEN LINE) ON FRONT ONLY.

*Enlarging grid patterns, page 13.
Using hot glue, page 14.*

Black Cat, Junglecat & Bunny

The domestic cat, with its nine lives, has an illustrious history that dates back nearly 3,500 years to ancient Egypt. On a spooky Halloween night, the shadowy black cat, with shining eyes and a highly developed sense of smell, roams the streets and alleys in search of treats. The junglecat and the adorable bunny live deep in the woods far away from humans. On Halloween night, they venture out of their dense forest habitat looking for adventure and something to add to their usual diet of rodents and carrots.

SAFETY TIP

Make tails for cats short enough to prevent tripping.

TAILS FOR CATS

Roll up a long piece of Polarfleece, hotglue closed, and handsew to the bottom back.

WHAT YOU NEED

Size (approximate age in years)	Small (3-4)	Medium (6-8)	Large (10-12)
Each costume: Polarfleece for coveralls, helmet, spats, and mittens, 60" (150cm) wide:	2¾ yds. (2.60m)	3⅜ yds. (3.10m)	3⅝ yds. (3.40m)

Other supplies for each costume:
- ❏ long zipper for front
- ❏ elastic for spats
- ❏ polyester fiberfill
- ❏ sewing machine
- ❏ needle and thread
- ❏ hot glue gun and glue sticks for the bags

For Black Cat:
- ❏ small piece of white Polarfleece or felt for decorations

For Junglecat:
- ❏ piece of contrasting fabric for ears, mittens, tail, and bag

For Bunny:
- ❏ piece of pink Polarfleece for tail, ears, and mittens
- ❏ piece of orange felt and a piece of green Polarfleece for treat bag decoration

BALACLAVA HELMET
Pattern, page 55 (double-layered version).

Stitch sides of ears, stuff with fiberfill, and handsew to the helmet. Trim Black Cat ears as shown.

COVERALLS

Stitch zipper on front. Stitch inner leg seams. Turn one leg right side out and push into the other leg. Stitch center seam from zipper end to neck edge. Stitch underarm seams. Stitch sleeves to armholes.

PINK POMPOM TAIL FOR BUNNY
See pompom for Gnome hat, page 48.

MITTENS
Pattern, page 49.

For each cat, hotglue spots for pads as shown.

SPATS
Pattern, page 87.

TREAT BAGS
For Black Cat or Bunny, use pattern on page 71. For Junglecat, use pattern on page 19.

Black Cat bag:
Decorate as desired.

Junglecat bag:
Omit drawstring. Cut one handle from Polarfleece. Hotglue everything. Decorate as desired.

Bunny bag:
Cut a carrot from orange felt and add accent lines with a black pen or marker. Cut a large leaf from green Polarfleece. Cut narrow fringe along the stretchy cross-grain width. Pull the fringe to curl it. Hotglue the carrot and leaf to the bag.

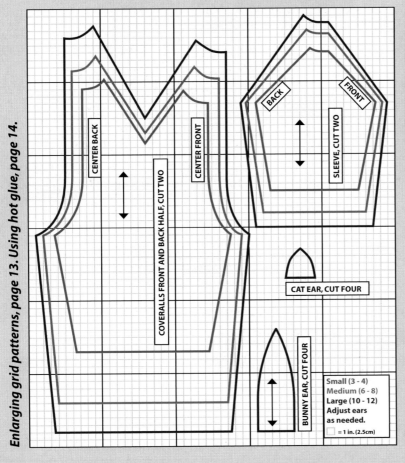

Enlarging grid patterns, page 13. Using hot glue, page 14.

CENTER BACK

COVERALLS FRONT AND BACK HALF, CUT TWO

CENTER FRONT

BACK

FRONT

SLEEVE, CUT TWO

CAT EAR, CUT FOUR

BUNNY EAR, CUT FOUR

Small (3 - 4)
Medium (6 - 8)
Large (10 - 12)
Adjust ears as needed.

☐ = 1 in. (2.5cm)

Apprentice Clown

This charming little clown is just a beginner and is still trying to learn the tricks of the trade.

GIANT COVERALLS

Stitch inner leg seams. Stitch center seam. Stitch sleeves to bodice. Stitch sides and underarms. Sew wide bias binding around neck edge to make a casing and insert elastic. Hem sleeve ends and leg ends. On inside, stitch stretched elastic around wrists to make ruffles. Handsew pompoms to front for mock buttons.

WHAT YOU NEED

Size (approximate age in years)→	Small (3-4)	Medium (6-8)	Large (10-12)
Medium-weight colorful cotton-type fabric, 45" (140cm) wide:	2¾ yds. (2.60m)	4¼ yds. (4.00m)	4¾ yds. (4.40m)
Polarfleece for neck ruffles in two contrasting colors, 60" (150cm) wide, each:	½ yd. (0.50m)	1 yd. (1.00m)	1 yd. (1.00m)

Other supplies:
- ❑ wide bias binding for neck edge
- ❑ narrow elastic for neck edge and sleeve end ruffles
- ❑ sewing machine   ❑ needle and thread
- ❑ wig

For pompoms:
- ❑ small piece of colorful Polarfleece
- ❑ polyester fiberfill

For treat container:
- ❑ large rectangular water jug
- ❑ Polarfleece to cover the jug
- ❑ colorful Polarfleece scraps for decorations
- ❑ hot glue gun and glue sticks

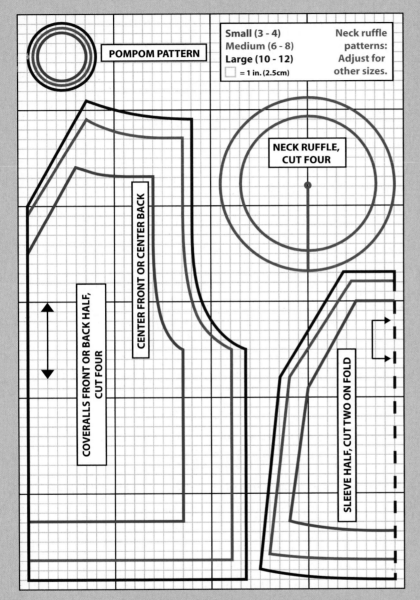

POMPOM PATTERN

Small (3 - 4)
Medium (6 - 8)
Large (10 - 12)
☐ = 1 in. (2.5cm)

Neck ruffle patterns: Adjust for other sizes.

NECK RUFFLE, CUT FOUR

COVERALLS FRONT OR BACK HALF, CUT FOUR

CENTER FRONT OR CENTER BACK

SLEEVE HALF, CUT TWO ON FOLD

Enlarging grid patterns, page 13. Using hot glue, page 14.

POMPOM FROM POLARFLEECE

Using a long needle and strong thread, baste all around the circular edge, pull to create a pouch, and stuff with fiberfill. Pull the thread tightly and sew the pompom closed.

NECK RUFFLE FROM POLARFLEECE

For each, cut four circles. Slit each from edge to center and cut out a dime-size piece at the center. Stitch or hotglue the eight slit edges end-to-end, joining the last edge to the first one to create a circle with a rolling outer edge. Adjust neck opening to fit over head.

TREAT CONTAINER

Cut and discard top from a large water jug. Cover with Polarfleece. Cut a long strip from Polarfleece for a handle, hotglue in half lengthwise and then hotglue the ends in place. Use colorful Polarfleece scraps to create a clown face, neck ruffle, and curly hair, hotgluing all. To make the hair from a piece of Polarfleece, cut one edge into a fringe along the stretchy cross-grain and pull to curl the ends.

Clown & Baby Clown

By exaggerating ordinary situations, clowns use their antics and absurd reactions to make audiences laugh.

JACKET
Pattern, page 123.

Round off corners of lower front. Press each sleeve-end ruffle in half lengthwise, right side out, gather raw edges, and stitch under sleeve ends of jacket. On outside, hotglue Polarfleece strips around sleeve ends.

PANTS
Pattern, page 28.

Trim leg ends with cotton print. On inside, stitch stretched elastic around ankles to make ruffles. Push wire through waist-band, forming a large stiff circle. Fold and hotglue suspenders lengthwise triple-layered, hotglue ends under waistband at front and back, crisscrossing at back. Cut stars and mock buttons from Polarfleece scraps and hotglue to the costume.

SHIRT
Pattern, page 17 (without lacy front panel).

Stitch bias binding around neck edge to make a casing and insert elastic. Hem sleeve ends. On inside, stitch stretched elastic around wrists to make ruffles.

WHAT YOU NEED

	Size (approximate age in years)→	Small (3-4)	Medium (6-8)	Large (10-12)
Clown:	Blue Polarfleece for jacket and treat bag, 60" (150cm) wide:	1 yd. (1.00m)	1⅝ yds. (1.50m)	1¾ yds. (1.60m)
	Red Polarfleece for pants, 60" (150cm) wide	1 yd. (1.00m)	1⅛ yds. (1.10m)	1⅜ yds. (1.30m)
	Yellow Polarfleece for suspenders, 60" (150cm) wide:	¼ yd. (0.25m)	½ yd. (0.50m)	½ yd. (0.50m)
	Colorful cotton print for trimming leg ends, and for sleeve end ruffles, 45" (115cm) wide:	½ yd. (0.50m)	⅝ yd. (0.60m)	⅝ yd. (0.60m)
	Cotton print for shirt: 45" (115cm) wide:	1½ yds. (1.40m)	2¼ yds. (2.10m)	2½ yds. (2.30m)

Other supplies for Clown:
- ❑ narrow elastic for shirt and leg end ruffles
- ❑ wig   ❑ bias binding
- ❑ 16-gauge galvanized wire for waistband
- ❑ wire cutters   ❑ two fake flowers
- ❑ double-sided foam tape
- ❑ hot glue gun and glue sticks
- ❑ sewing machine   ❑ needle and thread

For bows and shoe-tops:
- ❑ fabric scraps
- ❑ narrow elastic

For top hat:
- ❑ stiff cardboard
- ❑ black felt

For Baby Clown:
- ❑ yellow Polarfleece for headband and cape, 1 yd. of 60" wide (1.00m of 150cm wide)
- ❑ colorful Polarfleece scraps for trimmings
- ❑ hot glue gun and glue sticks

BOWS

Fold each bow in half, fabric and lining together, and stitch all three raw sides closed. Cut corners, slash opening at back, and turn right side out. Put the smaller bow on top of the larger one, wrap with a fabric scrap, and hotglue. Handsew elastic at back for a neckband.

SHOE-TOPS

Cut elastic to fit loosely around ankle and knot ends together to make a loop. Fold shoe-top in half with elastic loop in between and hotglue closed. Add mock shoelaces. Slip on and attach to shoe with double-sided foam tape.

TOP HAT

Hotglue black felt to cardboard. Cut out crown and brim. Roll crown into a tube and hotglue to the brim. Add a flower. Attach to wig with double-sided foam tape.

TREAT BAG
Pattern, page 71.

Cut only one handle as shown. Cut a large flower from Polarfleece scraps and hotglue to the bag.

baby clown

HEADBAND

Fold a piece of Polarfleece into a large headband and hotglue closed. Make a bow from fabric scraps and hotglue to the headband. Add curly Polarfleece strings (see Pumpkin, page 130).

CAPE

Cut a large circle from Polarfleece. Cut out a neck opening. Cut decorations from contrasting Polarfleece and hotglue to the cape.

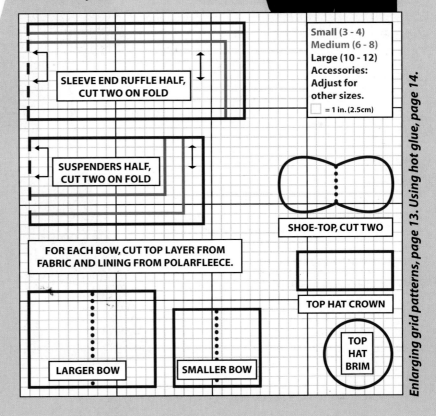

SLEEVE END RUFFLE HALF, CUT TWO ON FOLD

SUSPENDERS HALF, CUT TWO ON FOLD

FOR EACH BOW, CUT TOP LAYER FROM FABRIC AND LINING FROM POLARFLEECE.

LARGER BOW

SMALLER BOW

SHOE-TOP, CUT TWO

TOP HAT CROWN

TOP HAT BRIM

Small (3 - 4)
Medium (6 - 8)
Large (10 - 12)
Accessories:
Adjust for
other sizes.

☐ = 1 in. (2.5cm)

Enlarging grid patterns, page 13. Using hot glue, page 14.

Pierrot

The melancholy Pierrot, a French pantomime, is based on Pedrolino, a character in Italian *commedia dell'arte*. Wearing a traditional costume with a white face and a tear on the cheek, Pierrot has been transformed into a naive and appealing clown who charms everyone.

SHIRT & PANTS

Pattern for shirt, page 17 (without lacy front panel). Pattern for pants, page 28.

Cut half of the costume from black and half from white as shown. Stitch center front and center back seams of shirt. Then follow the sewing directions on pattern pages. Hem sleeve ends and leg ends. On inside, stitch stretched elastic around wrists and ankles to make ruffles. Stitch wide bias binding around neck to make a casing and insert elastic.

CAP

Stitch the four side slits closed. Sew wide bias binding to lower edge to make a casing. Insert elastic to fit comfortably around the head.

NECK RUFFLE

Stitch ends together. Trim lower edge with black bias binding. Sew wide bias binding around neck edge to make a casing and insert elastic.

WHAT YOU NEED

Size (approximate age in years)→	Small (3-4)	Medium (6-8)	Large (10-12)
Black lining satin, 55" (140cm) wide:	1¾ yds. (1.60m)	2¼ yds. (2.10m)	2¾ yds. (2.60m)
White lining satin, 55" (140cm) wide:	1¾ yds. (1.60m)	2¼ yds. (2.10m)	2¾ yds. (2.60m)

Other supplies:
- ❏ piece of hot pink lining satin for heart decorations
- ❏ narrow elastic for cap, shirt, leg ends, and neck ruffle
- ❏ one package of narrow black bias binding for neck ruffle
- ❏ one package of wide white bias binding for neck edge and cap
- ❏ sewing machine
- ❏ needle and thread

- ❏ polyester fiberfill for hearts
- ❏ wide elastic for waist

For treat bag:
- ❏ black fabric
- ❏ fabric scraps
- ❏ crayons
- ❏ polyester fiberfill
- ❏ hot glue gun and glue sticks

HEARTS

With right sides facing, stitch two layers together around all edges. Trim seam allowances and clip corners. Slash a small slit at center back and turn right side out. Stuff with fiberfill and handsew the slit closed. Sew the hearts to the costume as shown.

TREAT BAG
Pattern, page 71.

Decorate the bag with a little Pierrot face (double-layered and stuffed) and a neck ruffle, sewn or hotglued. Add facial details with crayons.

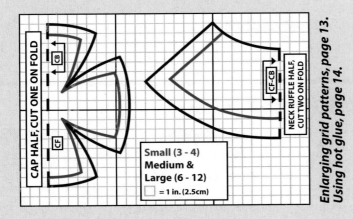

CAP HALF, CUT ONE ON FOLD

CB

CF

CF-CB

NECK RUFFLE HALF, CUT TWO ON FOLD

Small (3 - 4)
Medium &
Large (6 - 12)
☐ = 1 in. (2.5cm)

Enlarging grid patterns, page 13.
Using hot glue, page 14.

Jester & Baby Jester

Dressed in multicolored cheery costumes, jesters (or jokers) were kept at court by medieval rulers for amusing entertainment.

HAT

Pin the three sections together at headtop seams. Stitch, creating a large triangle with a hole at center. Stitch the side seams together, each color separately. Stitch the headband ends together. Fold the band in half lengthwise and stitch to the hat around the center hole. Stuff tips lightly with fiberfill. Sew a bell on each tip.

COLLAR

Hotglue the two layers together around edges.

TOP AND PANTS

Pattern, page 21.

MITTENS

Pattern, page 49.

WHAT YOU NEED

Size (approximate age in years)→	Small (3-4)	Medium (6-8)	Large (10-12)
Purple Polarfleece for pants and hat, 60" (150cm) wide:	1¼ yds. (1.20m)	1½ yds. (1.40m)	1¾ yds. (1.60m)
Orange Polarfleece for top, spats, and hat, 60" (150cm) wide:	1⅝ yds. (1.50m)	2⅜ yds. (2.20m)	2¾ yds. (2.60m)
Green Polarfleece for collar, mittens, treat bag & hat, 60" (150cm) wide:	1¼ yds. (1.20m)	1½ yds. (1.40m)	1½ yds. (1.40m)

Other supplies:
- ❏ wide elastic for waist
- ❏ three bells for hat
- ❏ sewing machine
- ❏ hot glue gun and glue sticks
- ❏ one bag of polyester fiberfill
- ❏ narrow elastic for spats
- ❏ needle and thread

For Baby Jester:
- ❏ purple Polarfleece, ⅞ yd. of 60" wide (0.80m of 150cm wide)
- ❏ yellow Polarfleece, ⅜ yd. of 60" wide (0.40m of 150cm wide)
- ❏ hot glue gun and glue sticks
- ❏ sewing machine
- ❏ needle and thread

SPATS
Pattern, page 43.

FINAL TOUCH

Cut diamond shapes from contrasting Polarfleece and hotglue to the costume as desired. Trim spats and collar with pompoms (page 91).

NO-SEW TREAT BAG

Cut a large circle from Polarfleece, piecing leftover fabric together. Cut diamond shapes from contrasting Polarfleece and hotglue to the bag. Cut holes around top edge. Weave a Polarfleece strip through holes for a drawstring.

Enlarging grid patterns, page 13. Using hot glue, page 14.

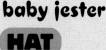
baby jester

CAPE

Cut a large circle from purple Polarfleece. Cut out a neck opening. Cut lower edge as shown. Cut diamond shapes from fabric scraps and hotglue to the cape as shown.

HAT

With wrong sides in, stitch the two layers together around face opening. Clip seam allowance. Stitch back seam of each of the two layers. Stitch the top piece to the hat. Topstitch lower edges together. Trim tips with pompoms (page 91). Decorate as shown.

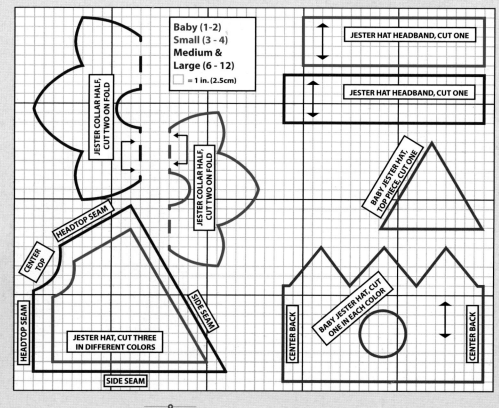

Baby (1-2)
Small (3 - 4)
Medium & Large (6 - 12)
☐ = 1 in. (2.5cm)

JESTER COLLAR HALF, CUT TWO ON FOLD

JESTER COLLAR HALF, CUT TWO ON FOLD

HEADTOP SEAM

CENTER TOP

HEADTOP SEAM

SIDE SEAM

JESTER HAT, CUT THREE IN DIFFERENT COLORS

SIDE SEAM

JESTER HAT HEADBAND, CUT ONE

JESTER HAT HEADBAND, CUT ONE

BABY JESTER HAT, TOP PIECE, CUT ONE

BABY JESTER HAT, CUT ONE IN EACH COLOR

CENTER BACK

CENTER BACK

97

Cinnamon Toast

Clowns wear a variety of creative costumes. This one is a big piece of toast walking down the street.

WHAT YOU NEED

(Adjust the size as needed)

Supplies:
- ☐ foam sheeting of ½ inch (12mm) thickness, 2 rolls of 36" (90cm) wide, total length, 100" (2.50m)
- ☐ long darning needle and strong thread
- ☐ one can of nontoxic brown water-soluble paint

For treat bag:
- ☐ black Polarfleece
- ☐ fabric scraps
- ☐ metallic glitter
- ☐ hot glue gun and glue sticks

COSTUME

Cut the pattern pieces out of foam. With right sides facing out and using a long needle and strong thread, handsew pieces together, leaving the entire bottom edge open for legs. Cut a face opening and holes for hands. On inside, sew the headtop piece from side to side so it goes over the head (as shown by dotted line in the pattern).

SPRAY-PAINT

Spray-paint the costume brown, spraying more paint at sides for crusty look. Spray-painting is best done outdoors. Protect the ground and your clothing. Let dry overnight.

TREAT BAG
Pattern, page 71.

Cut a mock shaker of cinnamon and sugar mix from fabric scraps and hotglue to the bag along with scattered glitter.

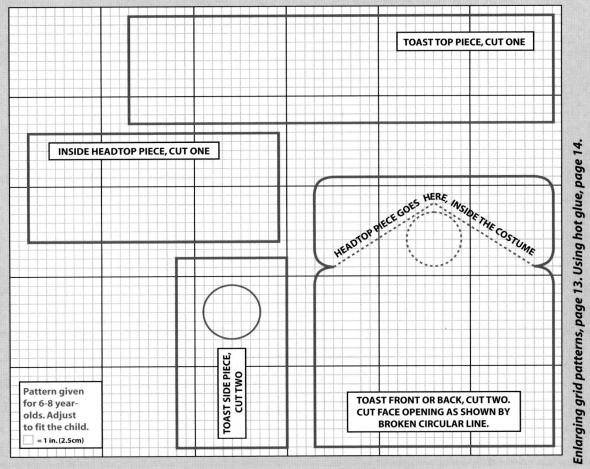

TOAST TOP PIECE, CUT ONE

INSIDE HEADTOP PIECE, CUT ONE

HEADTOP PIECE GOES HERE, INSIDE THE COSTUME

Pattern given for 6-8 year-olds. Adjust to fit the child.
☐ = 1 in. (2.5cm)

TOAST SIDE PIECE, CUT TWO

TOAST FRONT OR BACK, CUT TWO. CUT FACE OPENING AS SHOWN BY BROKEN CIRCULAR LINE.

Enlarging grid patterns, page 13. Using hot glue, page 14.

Ninja

Highly trained in the martial arts, a ninja is a member of a feudal Japanese society of secret agents. Children in the West are fascinated with the martial art characters they see in popular movies and cartoons.

 TOP AND PANTS
Pattern, page 21.

From metallic fabric, cut decorative patches for sleeve ends and top front. Baste the patches temporarily in place. From metallic fabric, cut a long sash to tie around waist and long strips to tie around ankles. Tuck a plastic sword under sash.

HELMET

Stitch center panel between the two side pieces, both layers separately. With right sides facing, stitch the two completed helmets together around front edge, including the flap, leaving lower edge open. Cut corners, clip curves, and turn right side out. Topstitch lower edges together. Stitch a piece of Velcro to flap ends.

FACESCARF

Cut one scarf from metallic fabric and one from Polarfleece for a comfortable lining. With right sides facing, stitch the straight top edges together. Turn right side out. Tie as shown.

WHAT YOU NEED

Size (approximate age in years)→	Small (3-4)	Medium (6-8)	Large (10-12)
Black Polarfleece for top, pants, helmet, facescarf lining, and treat bag, 60" (150cm) wide:	2⅛ yds. (2.00m)	3 yds. (2.70m)	3⅜ yds. (3.10m)
Metallic fabric, 45" (115cm) wide:	1 yd. (1.00m)	1 yd. (1.00m)	1 yd. (1.00m)

Other supplies:
❑ small piece of Velcro for helmet ❑ needle and thread ❑ cord for a drawstring
❑ plastic sword ❑ small piece of self-adhesive vinyl for treat bag decoration

 **NO-SEW SHORTCUT**

Wear a black sweatsuit inside out to hide any decorative details. Temporarily baste the decorations to the costume. Make a balaclava helmet, page 55, and hotglue the seams. Hotglue or handsew the lining to the facescarf.

 **TREAT BAG**
Pattern, page 59.

Draw a design such as a typical ninja posture or the yin-and-yang symbol on paper backing of self-adhesive vinyl. Cut it out, peel off the paper, and apply the decoration onto the bag.

Enlarging grid patterns, page 13. Using hot glue, page 14.

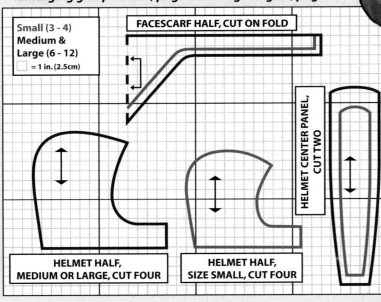

Small (3 - 4)
Medium &
Large (6 - 12)
☐ = 1 in. (2.5cm)

FACESCARF HALF, CUT ON FOLD

HELMET CENTER PANEL, CUT TWO

HELMET HALF, MEDIUM OR LARGE, CUT FOUR

HELMET HALF, SIZE SMALL, CUT FOUR

Knight

Knights were the medieval horse-riding soldiers who served in the European feudal system. They performed military duties in wars and expeditions, and guarded the castles of the nobility. Wearing splendid armor with protective coverings as a defense against weapons, they bravely encountered their enemies on the battlefield.

HOODED CLOAK

Cut the pattern parts for hood and cloak from both Polarfleece and metallic fabric. With metallic fabric between the Polarfleece layers, stitch center front and center back seams of hood. Again with metallic fabric between Polarfleece layers, stitch the cloak shoulder seams. Stitch hood to cloak around neck. On outside, topstitch the two layers together around face opening and lower edge. Create a crest from felt or crafting foam scraps. Hotglue the crest to cloak front.

 TOP AND PANTS
Pattern, page 21.

Fold the belt in half lengthwise, topstitch or hotglue closed, and attach one end to a buckle. Cut long strips from brown Polarfleece and wrap around legs. Tuck a plastic sword under belt.

WHAT YOU NEED

Size (approximate age in years)→	Small (3-4)	Medium (6-8)	Large (10-12)
Brown Polarfleece for hooded cloak, top, pants, belt, handguards, and treat bag, 60" (150cm) wide:	3 yds. (2.70m)	3½ yds. (3.10m)	4 yds. (3.60m)
Metallic silver net fabric for top layer of hooded cloak and handguards, 45" (115cm) wide:	1 yd. (1.00m)	1 yd. (1.00m)	1 yd. (1.00m)

Other supplies:
- ❑ wide elastic for waist
- ❑ plastic sword
- ❑ felt or crafting foam scraps for crest
- ❑ sewing machine
- ❑ buckle for belt
- ❑ hot glue gun and glue sticks
- ❑ needle and thread
- ❑ narrow elastic for handguards

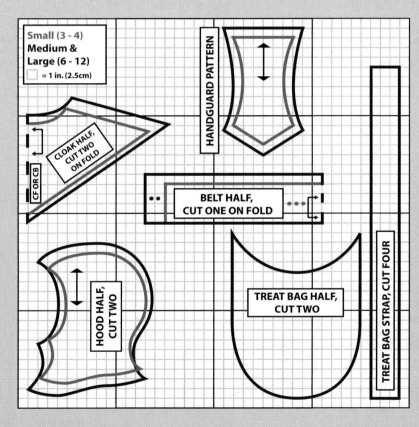

HANDGUARDS

For each, cut two layers from Polarfleece and one from metallic fabric. With metallic fabric between the two Polarfleece layers, stitch sides. Turn right side out. On inside, sew two loops from elastic to hook the handguard over thumb and middle finger.

TREAT BAG

Stitch strap ends together at center top and center bottom, each two separately. With wrong sides together, stitch the double-layered strap between bag front and back, creating a shoulder strap at the same time. On right side, topstitch the shoulder strap edges closed.

Enlarging grid patterns, page 13.
Using hot glue, page 14.

Geisha

A Japanese geisha is highly trained in music, dance, and literature. She is a respected companion with a rich tradition dating back hundreds of years, and excels in playing the samisen.

HAT

Stitch side seam and rounded top edge. Turn right side out. Stuff top lightly with fiberfill to make a bun. On outside, tie a strip of black Polarfleece loosely underneath the bun. Fold bottom edge under. Gather front edge vertically and handsew closed for a mock hairdo. Decorate with ribbons, flowers, and chopsticks (or pencils wrapped with paper or ribbon).

KIMONO
Pattern, page 27.

Cut the kimono from Polarfleece with center back on fold, adjusting the sleeve length for the child. Stitch sides and underarms. Trim sleeve ends and front edges with folded strip of black Polarfleece. Hem lower edge.

OBI

Cut two pattern pieces from Polarfleece to make a soft padding and hotglue together around edges. Cover with decorative fabric, hotgluing edges under. To attach ends at back, add Velcro or Polarfleece strips for ties. Knot two long decorative ribbons together on center front and tie ends together on top of obi at back. From leftover fabrics, sew a large, flat bow and pin at back to cover tie ends.

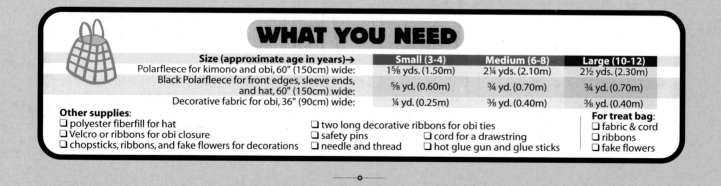

WHAT YOU NEED

Size (approximate age in years)→	Small (3-4)	Medium (6-8)	Large (10-12)
Polarfleece for kimono and obi, 60" (150cm) wide:	1⅝ yds. (1.50m)	2¼ yds. (2.10m)	2½ yds. (2.30m)
Black Polarfleece for front edges, sleeve ends, and hat, 60" (150cm) wide:	⅝ yd. (0.60m)	¾ yd. (0.70m)	¾ yd. (0.70m)
Decorative fabric for obi, 36" (90cm) wide:	¼ yd. (0.25m)	⅜ yd. (0.40m)	⅜ yd. (0.40m)

Other supplies:
- ❏ polyester fiberfill for hat
- ❏ Velcro or ribbons for obi closure
- ❏ chopsticks, ribbons, and fake flowers for decorations
- ❏ two long decorative ribbons for obi ties
- ❏ safety pins
- ❏ needle and thread
- ❏ cord for a drawstring
- ❏ hot glue gun and glue sticks

For treat bag:
- ❏ fabric & cord
- ❏ ribbons
- ❏ fake flowers

SAFETY TIP

For a small child, cut the kimono short enough to prevent tripping.

 **NO-SEW SHORTCUT**

Hotglue everything.

TREAT BAG
Pattern, page 69.

Insert a cord through casing for a drawstring. Decorate the bag with flowers and ribbons.

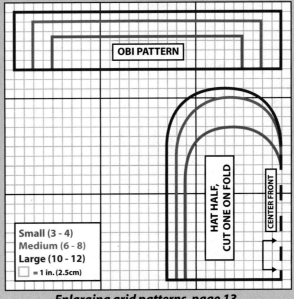

OBI PATTERN

HAT HALF, CUT ONE ON FOLD

CENTER FRONT

Small (3 - 4)
Medium (6 - 8)
Large (10 - 12)
☐ = 1 in. (2.5cm)

Enlarging grid patterns, page 13.
Using hot glue, page 14.

Gypsy

Gypsies or Roma, originally from India, now live in many countries. Ignoring national boundaries, they are seasonal nomads following ancient tribal links. With the strict laws and rituals of a rich culture that dates back to ancient times, they have their own language, Romany, and are known for their beautiful music, dancing, and traditional costumes.

SCARF AND SASH

From lurex, cut a large square scarf. Sew gold rickrack around edges. Tie the scarf around the head. Tie leftover piece around waist for a sash.

BLOUSE
Use shirt pattern, page 17.

VEST

With right sides together, stitch lining to vest around armholes and all edges except shoulders, leaving an opening at lower edge of center back. Trim corners, clip curves, and turn right side out. Stitch shoulder seams. Slipstitch hem opening closed. Trim with decorative ribbons.

NO-PATTERN SKIRT

Cut skirt as long and wide as desired. Stitch sides. Fit a piece of elastic around waist and stitch ends together for a waistband. Gather waist edge of fabric and zigzag the elastic waistband to skirt. Hem lower edge.

WHAT YOU NEED

Size (approximate age in years)→	Small (3-4)	Medium (6-8)	Large (10-12)
Metallic knit fabric (lurex) or similar for scarf and sash:	1 yd. (1.00m)	1 yd. (1.00m)	1 yd. (1.00m)
Fabric for blouse, 45" (115cm) wide:	1½ yds. (1.40m)	2¼ yds. (2.10m)	2½ yds. (2.30m)
Fabric for vest, 45" (115cm) wide:	½ yd. (0.50m)	⅝ yd. (0.60m)	¾ yd. (0.70m)
Fabric for vest lining, 45" (115cm) wide:	½ yd. (0.50m)	⅝ yd. (0.60m)	¾ yd. (0.70m)
Lace for blouse neck, front, and sleeve ends:	3½ yds. (3.10m)	4 yds. (3.50m)	4½ yds. (4.00m)

Other supplies:
- ❏ fabric for wide skirt (twice the skirt length)
- ❏ gold rickrack for scarf
- ❏ wide black elastic for waistband
- ❏ sewing machine   ❏ needle and thread

- ❏ narrow elastic for neck edge, sleeve ends, and earrings
- ❏ decorative ribbon for vest
- ❏ gold cord and two pretty buttons for earrings
- ❏ hot glue gun and glue sticks for earrings

For treat bag:
- ❏ fabric
- ❏ lace
- ❏ cord for a drawstring

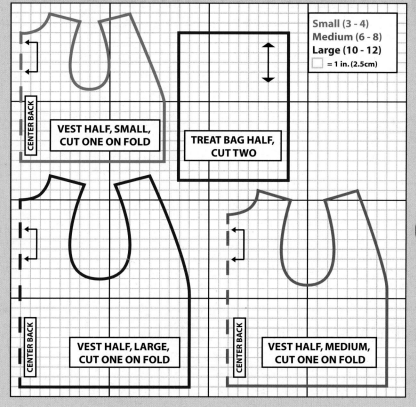

Small (3 - 4)
Medium (6 - 8)
Large (10 - 12)
☐ = 1 in. (2.5cm)

CENTER BACK

VEST HALF, SMALL,
CUT ONE ON FOLD

TREAT BAG HALF,
CUT TWO

CENTER BACK

VEST HALF, LARGE,
CUT ONE ON FOLD

CENTER BACK

VEST HALF, MEDIUM,
CUT ONE ON FOLD

EARRINGS

Make big earrings from gold cord and buttons, hotgluing all. Add elastic loops to go around ears.

SAFETY TIP

For a small child, cut the skirt short enough to prevent tripping.

TREAT BAG

Stitch side seams and bottom closed. Turn upper edge under and stitch closed to make a casing. Sew ruffled lace to top edge of casing. On outside, cut a hole in the casing and insert a cord for a drawstring.

Enlarging grid patterns, page 13.
Using hot glue, page 14.

Sheik & Bedouin

A sheik is a powerful patriarch of an Arabic tribe with a magnificent sheikdom under his rule. His beautiful palace is surrounded by exotic palm trees.

Bedouins, the nomadic Arabs of the desert, tend to their animal herds, riding camels fearlessly through vicious sandstorms and living in huge tents with their families. Their traditional desert clothing protects them from relentless heat by day and bitter cold by night.

sheik costume

LONG ROBE

Stitch sides and underarms. Cut wide bands from gold metallic fabric and hotglue decorative ribbon at center. Hotglue the bands to the robe at top front, lower side edges, and sleeve ends as shown. Hotglue decorative cord to cover the raw edges of bands.

HEAD COVER

Place a large square piece of fabric on head as shown. Wrap and tie the cord around head.

TREAT BAG

Pattern, page 119.

WARM TOUCH

For cold weather, make neck warmer (shown on Bedouin) and arm warmers (not shown) from Polarfleece, see pages 30-31.

SAFETY TIP

For a small child, cut the robe short enough to prevent tripping.

WHAT YOU NEED (SHEIK)

Size (approximate age in years)→	Small (3-4)	Medium (6-8)	Large (10-12)
Polarfleece for robe, 60" (150cm) wide:	2 yds. (1.80m)	2⅓ yds. (2.10m)	2⅝ yds. (2.40m)
Velour or similar fabric for head cover:	1 yd. (1.00m)	1 yd. (1.00m)	1 yd. (1.00m)

Other supplies:
- ❑ cord for head cover, 2 yds. (1.80m)
- ❑ hot glue gun and glue sticks

For trimming the robe:
- ❑ gold metallic fabric
- ❑ decorative ribbon
- ❑ decorative cord

For treat bag:
- ❑ fancy fabric
- ❑ tassel

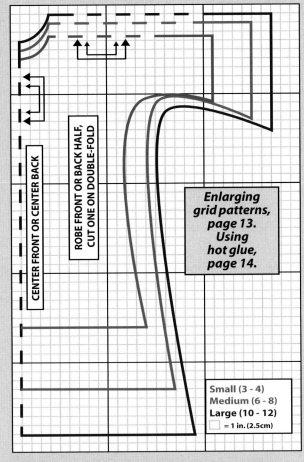

CENTER FRONT OR CENTER BACK

ROBE FRONT OR BACK HALF, CUT ONE ON DOUBLE-FOLD

Enlarging grid patterns, page 13. Using hot glue, page 14.

Small (3 - 4)
Medium (6 - 8)
Large (10 - 12)
☐ = 1 in. (2.5cm)

— bedouin costume —

LONG ROBE

Stitch sides and underarms. Slit upper and lower edge of front as shown. Trim raw edges of slits and neck edge with bias binding. Hem sleeve ends and lower edge.

HEAD COVER

Place a large square piece of fabric on head as shown. Cut a long strip from black fabric, wrap and tie around head.

MUSTACHE

Create a mustache from craft hair and attach with spirit gum or self-adhesive, rolled bandage.

TREAT BAG

Pattern, page 50.

Cut a palm tree and coconuts from fabric scraps and hotglue to the bag.

NO-SEW VERSION
for both.

Make the robes from Polarfleece. Hotglue seams.

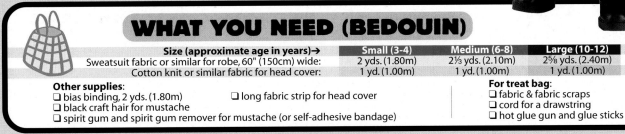

WHAT YOU NEED (BEDOUIN)

Size (approximate age in years)→	Small (3-4)	Medium (6-8)	Large (10-12)
Sweatsuit fabric or similar for robe, 60" (150cm) wide:	2 yds. (1.80m)	2⅓ yds. (2.10m)	2⅝ yds. (2.40m)
Cotton knit or similar fabric for head cover:	1 yd. (1.00m)	1 yd. (1.00m)	1 yd. (1.00m)

Other supplies:
❏ bias binding, 2 yds. (1.80m)
❏ black craft hair for mustache
❏ spirit gum and spirit gum remover for mustache (or self-adhesive bandage)
❏ long fabric strip for head cover

For treat bag:
❏ fabric & fabric scraps
❏ cord for a drawstring
❏ hot glue gun and glue sticks

Viking

Vikings, legendary Scandinavian pirates, were the best seafarers and shipbuilders of their time. One thousand years ago, a Viking warrior named Leif Ericson sailed to the shores of Eastern Canada. Icelandic sagas and excavations have revealed clues to their lifestyle, tools, ships, jewelry, and shelters.

TOP AND PANTS
Pattern, page 21.

HELMET

Stitch side and top seam. Turn right side out. Fold lower edge up three times for a wide band and hotglue closed. Stitch horn sides, stuff with fabric scraps, tuck lower edge in, and hotglue to the helmet. Roll up pieces of aluminum foil, shape as desired, and hotglue to helmet for mock rivets.

SPATS, SCABBARD, AND BELT

Hotglue spats double-layered around edges. Cut holes at back edges and attach Polarfleece strips for ties. Hotglue scabbard front to back along sides and bottom. Hotglue back top edge under for a large loop. Fold the belt in half lengthwise, hotglue closed, sew a piece of Velcro at back, and slip end through the belt loop. Decorate with fabric strips, all hotglued.

SHIELD

Make mock rivets to match the helmet. Twist aluminum foil into rope. Hotglue the rivets and rope to disposable pizza pan. Crinkle and then straighten a large sheet of foil. Place it over the pan, press around rivets and rope, and then press foil edges tightly under pan edges. (If foil tears, repair with foil hotglued on top. Use Polarfleece scrap to protect your hands.) Rub shoe polish over raised parts for patina. Cut a piece of Polarfleece for a handle and attach ends with duct tape to shield back.

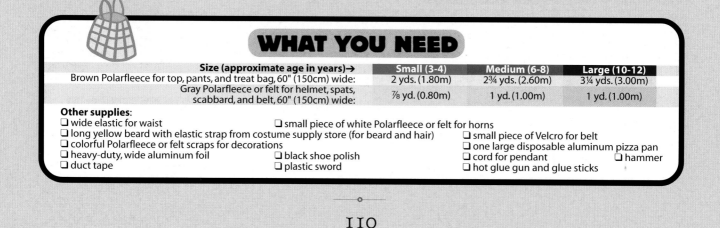

WHAT YOU NEED

Size (approximate age in years)→	Small (3-4)	Medium (6-8)	Large (10-12)
Brown Polarfleece for top, pants, and treat bag, 60" (150cm) wide:	2 yds. (1.80m)	2¾ yds. (2.60m)	3¼ yds. (3.00m)
Gray Polarfleece or felt for helmet, spats, scabbard, and belt, 60" (150cm) wide:	⅞ yd. (0.80m)	1 yd. (1.00m)	1 yd. (1.00m)

Other supplies:
- ❏ wide elastic for waist
- ❏ long yellow beard with elastic strap from costume supply store (for beard and hair)
- ❏ colorful Polarfleece or felt scraps for decorations
- ❏ heavy-duty, wide aluminum foil
- ❏ duct tape
- ❏ small piece of white Polarfleece or felt for horns
- ❏ black shoe polish
- ❏ plastic sword
- ❏ small piece of Velcro for belt
- ❏ one large disposable aluminum pizza pan
- ❏ cord for pendant
- ❏ hammer
- ❏ hot glue gun and glue sticks

BEARD AND HAIR

Trim the long beard to fit the child. Hotglue the trimmings under helmet rim for hair as shown.

PENDANT

Roll up a long piece of aluminum foil, twist into a rope and then into a loose knot. Hammer it flat and attach to a long cord.

 NO-SEW VERSION

Wear a brown sweatsuit turned inside out. Hotglue everything else.

TREAT BAG
Pattern, page 103.

Enlarging grid patterns, page 13. Using hot glue, page 14.

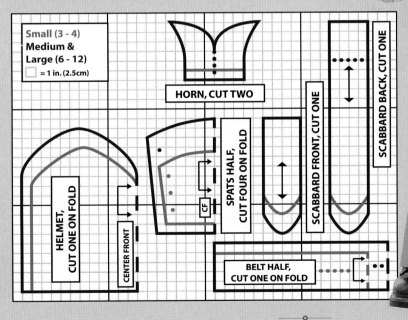

Small (3 - 4)
**Medium &
Large (6 - 12)**
☐ = 1 in. (2.5cm)

HORN, CUT TWO

HELMET, CUT ONE ON FOLD

CENTER FRONT

SPATS HALF, CUT FOUR ON FOLD

CF

SCABBARD FRONT, CUT ONE

SCABBARD BACK, CUT ONE

BELT HALF, CUT ONE ON FOLD

Hawaiian

The inhabitants of the exotic Hawaiian Islands mesmerize us with their music, dancing, and culture. They weave beautiful flowers and leaves into a traditional lei, a long garland worn around the neck and given as a token of welcome or farewell.

BODYSUIT

Pattern, page 45.

FLOWERS

For each, you'll need about 2 yds. (1.80m) of crepe paper streamer. Using a long needle and strong thread, baste along one edge of the paper. Gather tightly and tie thread ends together. Roll tight stamens from paper and hotglue several to the center of each flower. Hotglue flowers to hair clips, to elastic wristband over leaves cut from Polarfleece, and to the treat container.

LEI

You'll need about 40 yds. (37 meters) of crepe paper streamer. Using a long needle and strong thread, baste along the center of the streamer. Gather tightly as you go, and twist around and around. Tie thread ends securely together.

WHAT YOU NEED

Size (approximate age in years)→	Small (3-4)	Medium (6-8)
Spandex with two-way stretch for bodysuit, 60" (150cm) wide:	½ yd. (0.50m)	⅔ yd. (0.60m)
Green Polarfleece for waistband and treat container, 60" (150cm) wide:	⅓ yd. (0.30m)	⅓ yd. (0.30m)

Other supplies:
- ❑ brown tights
- ❑ long needle and strong thread
- ❑ three packages of green paper twist for skirt and treat container
- ❑ large rectangular water jug for treat container
- ❑ two rolls of crepe paper streamer for lei, additional colors for flowers
- ❑ hair clips
- ❑ elastic to make a wristband
- ❑ hot glue gun and glue sticks

SKIRT

Cut the waistband from Polarfleece. With long edges together, press in half to create a fold line. Open out waistband, wrong side up. Cut paper twist into lengths, twice the desired length of the finished skirt. Untwist and flatten each piece. With short edges together, press each piece in half to create a fold line. Aligning the fold lines, place the paper pieces side by side at right angles across the waistband, and hotglue in place. To create more fullness, add two more layers of paper pieces and hotglue in place. Refold the waistband in half, enclosing paper pieces, and hotglue closed. Cut the paper pieces lengthwise, from hem to waistband, to create fringe. Cut two long strips from leftover fabric, attach to waistband ends, and tie at side.

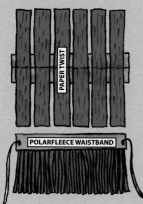

NO-SEW SHORTCUT

Buy a bodysuit. Everything else is hotglued and handsewn.

TREAT CONTAINER

Cut and discard top from a large water jug. Cover with Polarfleece. Cut a long wide strip from Polarfleece, hotglue in half lengthwise for a handle, and hotglue ends in place. Cut several pieces of green paper twist. Untwist and flatten each piece, cut lower ends into fringe, and hotglue upper ends around the rim.

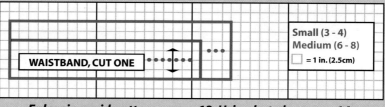

WAISTBAND, CUT ONE

Small (3 - 4)
Medium (6 - 8)
❑ = 1 in. (2.5cm)

Enlarging grid patterns, page 13. Using hot glue, page 14.

Pyramid

Monuments of a lost civilization, magnificent stone pyramids are the wonders of ancient Egypt. Built as burial tombs for great kings and pharaohs, these awe-inspiring enchanted structures hide a maze of underground passageways and inner chambers filled with treasures meant for the afterlife. Enter the most sacred parts of the pyramids at your own risk, as many would-be grave robbers have disappeared without a trace. Those able to escape have had mysterious curses cast upon them. Hieroglyphics, ancient Egyptian pictographic writing, is both symbolic and phonetic.

BASE ROBE

With wrong sides together, hotglue robe sides and underarms. On outside, hotglue wire to hem front and back. Cut two pyramids and hotglue to the robe front and back along the sides and hem, covering the wire.

WHAT YOU NEED

Size (approximate age in years)→	Small (3-4)	Medium (6-8)	Large (10-12)
Brown Polarfleece for base robe and headband, 60" (150cm) wide:	1½ yds. (1.40m)	1¾ yds. (1.60m)	2 yds. (1.80m)
Tan, tightly-woven, suede-like fabric for headscarf, pyramid, and treat bag, 55" (140cm) wide:	1¼ yds. (1.20m)	1½ yds. (1.40m)	1¾ yds. (1.60m)

Other supplies:
- ❑ 16-gauge galvanized wire for the robe hem and cobra, 2½ yds. (2.30m)
- ❑ wire cutters
- ❑ hot glue gun and glue sticks
- ❑ black permanent marker (fat tip)

Craft supplies to make a cobra for headband:
- ❑ crafting foam
- ❑ pipe cleaners
- ❑ felt

HEADSCARF

Cut two slits as shown. Cut the headband from Polarfleece and press it in half lengthwise. Hotglue the scarf center inside the folded headband, between slits, with scarf sides falling freely at each side. Create a fearsome cobra from crafting foam, pipe cleaners, felt, and wire, and hotglue to the headband. Tie at back.

FINAL TOUCH

With a black marker, divide the pyramids into big stone-like patches with uneven lines and rounded corners. Draw simple hieroglyphs on stones as shown.

 TREAT BAG
Pattern, page 19.

Stitch top edge under into a casing. Cut a long strip from leftover fabric, insert through casing for a drawstring, and knot ends together.

Enlarging grid patterns, page 13. Using hot glue, page 14.

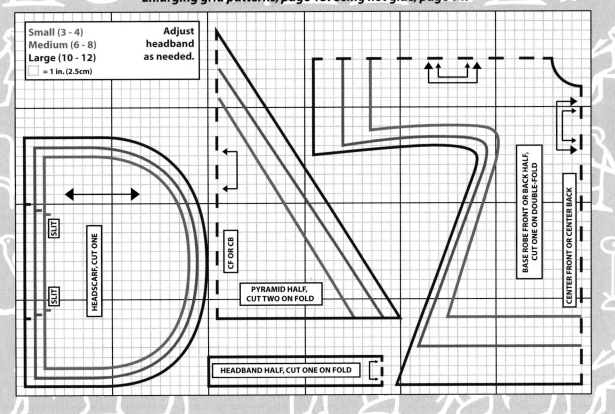

Small (3 - 4)
Medium (6 - 8)
Large (10 - 12)
☐ = 1 in. (2.5cm)

Adjust headband as needed.

SLIT

SLIT

HEADSCARF, CUT ONE

CF OR CB

PYRAMID HALF, CUT TWO ON FOLD

HEADBAND HALF, CUT ONE ON FOLD

BASE ROBE FRONT OR BACK HALF, CUT ONE ON DOUBLE-FOLD

CENTER FRONT OR CENTER BACK

Native Americans

When Columbus sailed to America, he believed he had landed in India, so he called the native inhabitants Indians. The misnomer remained and was eventually applied to almost all of the indigenous, non-European inhabitants who had lived in the Western Hemisphere for thousands of years. Their beautiful costumes vary by tribe and region. The Hollywood versions, popularized by movies and beloved by children, feature feathers, fringes, beadwork, and colorful intricate designs.

boy

TOP AND PANTS
Pattern, page 21.

Top: Cut hem and sleeve ends into fringe. Cut a piece of Polarfleece for a front panel, trim to match the neck edge, and hotglue in place. Hotglue a Polarfleece strip around the panel as shown. Slit the double-layered center top edge, cut holes in corners, and attach Polarfleece strips for ties. Cut two large rectangles for shoulder panels. Cut one edge into fringe, hotglue a contrasting band and rickrack to uncut edge. Hotglue the panels in place.

Pants: Cut leg ends into fringe. Cut two wide bands for sides. Cut one edge of each into fringe. Hotglue rickrack to bands. Hotglue the bands over side seams.

HEADDRESS

Fold the headband in half and hotglue closed with feathers in between. Decorate as desired. Hotglue a long Polarfleece strip to wrong side of headband, centering and leaving strip ends free. Tie strip ends behind head with band ends trailing freely at each side.

NO-SEW VERSION
for both.

Hotglue all seams. Cut holes around waist edge of pants and weave elastic through holes.

TREAT BAG
for both. Pattern, page 19.

Decorate with fabric scraps, all hotglued.

WHAT YOU NEED (BOY)

Size (approximate age in years)→	Small (3-4)	Medium (6-8)	Large (10-12)
Brown Polarfleece for top, pants, and treat bag, 60" (150cm) wide:	1⅞ yds. (1.80m)	2⅝ yds. (2.40m)	3 yds. (2.70m)
Red and green Polarfleece for decorations, 60" (150cm) wide, each:	¼ yd. (0.25m)	¼ yd. (0.25m)	¼ yd. (0.25m)
Tan Polarfleece for decorations, 60" (150cm) wide:	⅛ yd. (0.10m)	⅛ yd. (0.10m)	⅛ yd. (0.10m)
Other supplies:	❑ eleven feathers	❑ hot glue gun and glue sticks	

DRESS

Stitch sides and underarms. Cut hem and sleeve ends into fringe. Cut bands, rickrack, and triangles from contrasting Polarfleece and hotglue to the dress. Hotglue the front panel in place. Then hotglue a strip around it and loops on top, all cut from Polarfleece. Weave a long Polarfleece strip through the loops as shown. Fold the belt in half, hotglue closed, cut holes in each end, and attach Polarfleece strips to tie on front.

BOOTS

Stitch back seam of each four. With right sides facing, stitch each two together at upper edge. Turn right side out. Topstitch lower edges together. Cut two long strips from Polarfleece, handsew center to boot back, and wrap ends as shown.

EASY RICKRACK
Instructions, page 51.

HEADBAND

Fold the headband in half and hotglue closed with feathers in between. Overlap ends and sew a piece of Velcro for closure. Decorate as desired.

Enlarging grid patterns, page 13. Using hot glue, page 14.

CENTER FRONT OR BACK

DRESS FRONT OR BACK HALF, CUT ONE ON DOUBLE-FOLD

DRESS FRONT PANEL, CUT ONE

CENTER FRONT

BOOTS HALF, CUT FOUR ON FOLD

Small (3 - 4)
Medium (6 - 8)
Large (10 - 12)
Boots, front panel, and headband: Adjust as needed.

☐ = 1 in. (2.5cm)

BELT HALF, CUT ONE ON FOLD

GIRL, HEADBAND HALF ON FOLD

BOY, HEADBAND HALF ON FOLD

WHAT YOU NEED (GIRL)

Size (approximate age in years)→	Small (3-4)	Medium (6-8)	Large (10-12)
Tan Polarfleece for dress and boots, 60" (150cm) wide:	1⅝ yds. (1.50m)	2⅜ yds. (2.20m)	2½ yds. (2.30m)
Brown Polarfleece for decorations and treat bag, 60" (150cm) wide:	½ yd. (0.50m)	½ yd. (0.50m)	½ yd. (0.50m)
Orange Polarfleece for headband and decorations, 60" (150cm) wide:	¼ yd. (0.25m)	¼ yd. (0.25m)	¼ yd. (0.25m)
Red Polarfleece for decorations, 60" (150cm) wide:	⅛ yd. (0.10m)	⅛ yd. (0.10m)	⅛ yd. (0.10m)

Other supplies: ☐ small piece of Velcro for headband closure ☐ two feathers ☐ hot glue gun and glue sticks

Sultan

A sultan is a prince of noble lineage with the authority to rule the territories of a great empire. He lives in a fabulous palace and wears elegant caftans and turbans.

TURBAN

Pleat two opposite edges until each measures approximately 10" (25cm) long and stitch together for a front seam. Stitch top seam. Turn right side out. Fold lower edge under and hotglue in place.

BROOCH

Cut a diamond-shaped piece of cardboard. Decorate with fabric scraps, ribbons, and a fake gem or fancy button, and hotglue to the turban front over a feather.

LONG ROBE
Pattern and trimmings, page 109.

Hotglue ribbon around raw neck edge.

WARM TOUCH
Neck warmer and arm warmers (not shown in photo), pages 30-31.

SAFETY TIP

For a small child, cut the robe short enough to prevent tripping.

WHAT YOU NEED

Size (approximate age in years)→	Small (3-4)	Medium (6-8)	Large (10-12)
Metallic fabric for turban, robe trimmings, and treat bag, 36" (90cm) wide:	2 yds. (1.80m)	2 yds. (1.80m)	2 yds. (1.80m)
Velour or similar fabric for robe, 60" (150cm) wide:	2 yds. (1.80m)	2⅓ yds. (2.10m)	2⅝ yds. (2.40m)

Other supplies:
❑ ostrich feather ❑ decorative ribbon for trimming the robe as desired
❑ tassel ❑ hot glue gun and glue sticks

For brooch:
❑ piece of cardboard ❑ fabric scraps
❑ ribbons ❑ fake gem

🚫 NO-SEW SHORTCUT

Hotglue robe seams. Fuse foil gift wrap to front and sleeve ends, or use self-adhesive metallic vinyl. Fold a sheet of crisp gift wrap into a turban, attaching the folds and seams with double-sided foam tape. (Sneaky shortcut: Wrap a scarf around hat and attach with pins.)

TREAT BAG

With right sides together, stitch side seam closed. Stitch long edges of handle together and turn right side out. With right sides together and raw upper edges even, stitch handle ends to upper edge of bag. Turn upper edge under and hotglue or stitch in place. On inside, with top loop of the tassel between the fabric, gather and knot the bottom tightly closed with a strong piece of elastic, attaching the tassel end securely.

Enlarging grid patterns, page 13. Using hot glue, page 14.

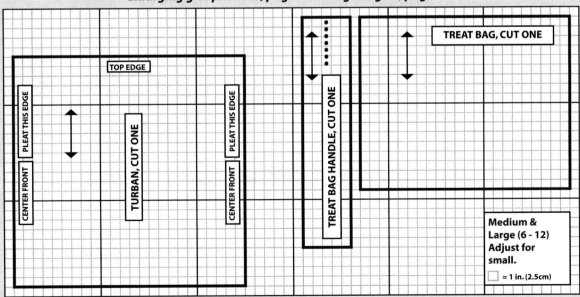

TOP EDGE

PLEAT THIS EDGE

CENTER FRONT

TURBAN, CUT ONE

PLEAT THIS EDGE

CENTER FRONT

TREAT BAG HANDLE, CUT ONE

TREAT BAG, CUT ONE

Medium & Large (6 - 12) Adjust for small.

☐ = 1 in. (2.5cm)

Cave Man & Cave Baby

Long beyond memory, our ancestors lived in caves. They squatted around hearth fires, safe from the cold and the dangers lurking in the darkness. Hunting for food and dressing in animal skins, they survived and kept warm. They used the bones and teeth of their prey as trophies to decorate their primitive costumes.

COSTUME

Cut small holes as shown at sides and top. Cut two long strips from Polarfleece and attach through the holes at sides. To wear the costume, push one of the side strips through the hole at top and tie the strips together at back.

HEADBAND

Overlap the ends and hotglue together. Fold the band triple-layered and hotglue closed. Cut two large bones from white Polarfleece. Hotglue edges together while stuffing with fabric scraps. Hotglue the bone to the headband.

WHAT YOU NEED

Size (approximate age in years)→ Animal print Polarfleece for costume, headband, and treat bag, 60" (150cm) wide:	Small (3-4)	Medium (6-8)	Large (10-12)
	⅞ yd. (0.80m)	1 yd. (1.00m)	1⅜ yds. (1.30m)

Other supplies:
- ❏ piece of white Polarfleece for bone decoration
- ❏ Polarfleece strip for necklace
- ❏ hot glue gun and glue sticks

Cave Baby:
- ❏ animal print Polarfleece for cape and headband, ⅞ yd. of 60" wide (0.80m of 150cm wide)
- ❏ piece of white Polarfleece for bone decoration
- ❏ Polarfleece strip for necklace
- ❏ hot glue gun and glue sticks

NECKLACE

From Polarfleece, cut a long strip for a necklace. Cut mock predator teeth from white Polarfleece and hotglue to the strip. Tie loosely around the neck.

TREAT BAG
Pattern, page 103.

Pattern, page 103.

cave baby

HEADBAND

Make a headband and decorate with a stuffed bone (see Cave Man).

CAPE AND NECKLACE

Cut a large circle from Polarfleece. Cut out a neck opening. Cut lower edge unevenly as shown. From Polarfleece, cut a long strip for a necklace. Hotglue one large mock tooth from white Polarfleece to the strip. Tie loosely around the neck.

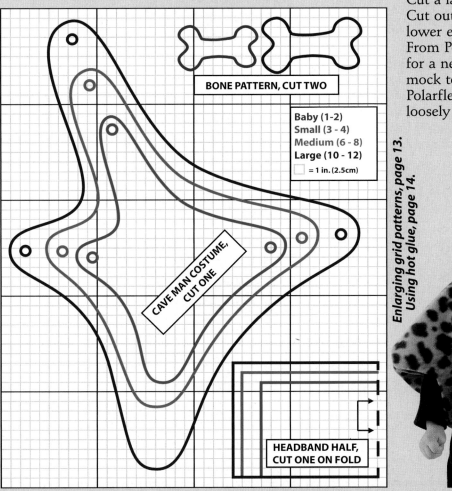

BONE PATTERN, CUT TWO

Baby (1-2)
Small (3 - 4)
Medium (6 - 8)
Large (10 - 12)
☐ = 1 in. (2.5cm)

CAVE MAN COSTUME, CUT ONE

HEADBAND HALF, CUT ONE ON FOLD

Enlarging grid patterns, page 13.
Using hot glue, page 14.

Enlarging grid patterns, page 13.
Using hot glue, page 14.

Scarecrow

A scarecrow, stuffed with straw and wearing ragged clothes, frightens away birds and other predators, discouraging them from devouring the delicious fruits and vegetables in your garden.

HAIR

Cut a piece of wide elastic to fit around head and sew ends together into a hairband. Tie strands of long raffia to the hairband and trim to desired length. Large straw hat covers the hairband with raffia falling down as hair.

JACKET

Stitch shoulders. Stitch sleeves to bodice. Stitch sides and underarms. Press front edges under. Cut buttonholes and sew on buttons.

WHAT YOU NEED

Size (approximate age in years)→	Small (3-4)	Medium (6-8)	Large (10-12)
Loosely-woven jute-type fabric for jacket, pants, and treat bag, 55" (140cm) wide:	2 yds. (1.80m)	2¾ yds. (2.60m)	3 yds. (2.70m)

Other supplies:
- ❏ colorful fabric scraps for trimmings
- ❏ large straw hat
- ❏ one package of straw-yellow paper twist
- ❏ wide elastic for hairband and waist
- ❏ 3-4 large buttons
- ❏ one bunch of long raffia for hair
- ❏ hot glue gun and glue sticks

 PANTS
Pattern, page 28.

🍒 FINAL TOUCH

Cut several patches from colorful fabric scraps and stitch or hotglue to the jacket and pants. Cut paper twist into pieces. Untwist and flatten the pieces, cut lower ends into fringe, and hotglue upper ends under sleeve ends and leg ends.

🚫 NO-SEW SHORTCUT

Hotglue all seams. Cut holes around the waist edge of pants and weave strong elastic through the holes. Or use an old pair of pants and jacket and decorate as shown.

📄 TREAT BAG
Pattern, page 71.

Cut simple scarecrow image and background details from fabric scraps and hotglue to the bag.

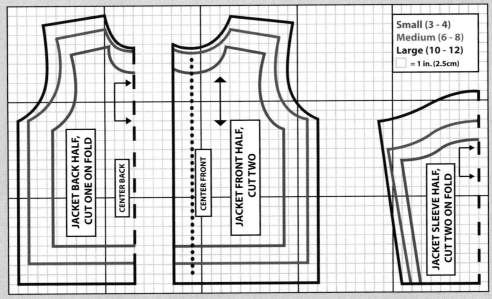

Small (3 - 4)
Medium (6 - 8)
Large (10 - 12)
☐ = 1 in. (2.5cm)

JACKET BACK HALF, CUT ONE ON FOLD

CENTER BACK

CENTER FRONT

JACKET FRONT HALF, CUT TWO

JACKET SLEEVE HALF, CUT TWO ON FOLD

Enlarging grid patterns, page 13. Using hot glue, page 14.

Cowboy & Cowgirl

Immortalized in popular Western movies, the cowboys of American folklore were heroic ranch workers in the legendary Wild West. They rode on horseback, rounding up huge herds of cattle for branding, selecting ones for market, and driving them to the nearest railroad town.

cowboy

VEST
Pattern, page 107.

Stitch or hotglue shoulder seams.

TREAT BAG
Pattern, page 50.

Create a cactus from felt and stiff ribbon and hotglue to the bag.

CHAPS AND BELT

Cut two pieces for fringe-bands, each the length of the side seam and about 6" (15cm) wide. Press each in half lengthwise, right side out. With right sides together, pin chaps front to back with bands between sides and all four raw edges even. Stitch side seams through all thicknesses. Cut the fringe-bands into fringe. Press belt loops triple-folded, stitch closed, fold in half, and stitch under top edge of chaps at front, back, and sides. Sew pieces of Velcro between inner leg seams. On outside, hotglue decorative ribbon over side seams. Press the belt in half lengthwise, stitch closed, and attach one end to a buckle.

WHAT YOU NEED (COWBOY)

Size (approximate age in years)→	Small (3-4)	Medium (6-8)	Large (10-12)
Cowhide-print Polarfleece for vest, 60" (150cm) wide:	½ yd. (0.50m)	⅝ yd. (0.60m)	¾ yd. (0.70m)
Fake suede-like fabric for chaps, fringe-bands, belt, and belt loops, 55" (140cm) wide:	1 yd. (1.00m)	1⅓ yds. (1.20m)	1⅝ yds. (1.50m)

Other supplies:
- ❑ old hat, shirt, and bandanna
- ❑ belt buckle ❑ sewing machine
- ❑ hot glue gun and glue sticks

For chaps:
- ❑ Velcro for inner leg seam closure
- ❑ decorative ribbon for trimming the side seams

For treat bag:
- ❑ heavy white cotton fabric
- ❑ cord for a drawstring
- ❑ piece of green felt ❑ stiff black ribbon

WRAPAROUND MINISKIRT

Stitch fabric to lining, leaving an opening at left front edge. Trim corners, clip curves, turn right side out, and press. Add Velcro for waist edge closure.

SPATS

Fuse stiff interfacing to the wrong side of fabric. Stitch lining to fabric at top edge only. Trim corners, slash seam allowance of front slit, turn right side out, and press. Topstitch the loose edges together. Cut holes at back edges and attach cords to tie behind legs.

VEST

Pattern, page 107.

Line the vest with broadcloth.

TREAT BAG

Pattern, page 103.

FINAL TOUCH

Decorate the vest, miniskirt, spats, and treat bag with ribbons, felt scraps, and tassels, all hotglued.

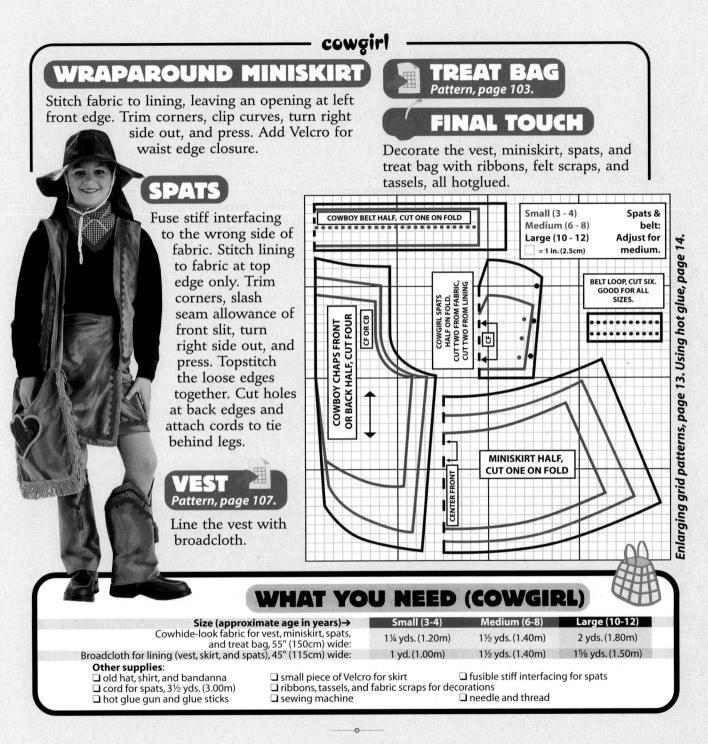

COWBOY BELT HALF, CUT ONE ON FOLD

Small (3 - 4)
Medium (6 - 8)
Large (10 - 12)
☐ = 1 in. (2.5cm)

Spats & belt: Adjust for medium.

BELT LOOP, CUT SIX. GOOD FOR ALL SIZES.

COWBOY CHAPS FRONT OR BACK HALF, CUT FOUR

CF OR CB

COWGIRL SPATS HALF ON FOLD, CUT TWO FROM FABRIC, CUT TWO FROM LINING

CF

MINISKIRT HALF, CUT ONE ON FOLD

CENTER FRONT

Enlarging grid patterns, page 13. Using hot glue, page 14.

WHAT YOU NEED (COWGIRL)

Size (approximate age in years)→	Small (3-4)	Medium (6-8)	Large (10-12)
Cowhide-look fabric for vest, miniskirt, spats, and treat bag, 55" (150cm) wide:	1¼ yds. (1.20m)	1½ yds. (1.40m)	2 yds. (1.80m)
Broadcloth for lining (vest, skirt, and spats), 45" (115cm) wide:	1 yd. (1.00m)	1½ yds. (1.40m)	1⅝ yds. (1.50m)

Other supplies:
☐ old hat, shirt, and bandanna
☐ cord for spats, 3½ yds. (3.00m)
☐ hot glue gun and glue sticks
☐ small piece of Velcro for skirt
☐ ribbons, tassels, and fabric scraps for decorations
☐ sewing machine
☐ fusible stiff interfacing for spats
☐ needle and thread

Flower & Tree

Afew brilliant flowers bloom just before the snow falls and winter grips the Northern Hemisphere. When fall arrives in the North, the rich green pigment in tree leaves breaks down, exposing all the brilliant hues of orange, yellow, and red. Without their green color, leaves fly away in the powerful wind, making the branches lighter, ready to hold the heavy winter snows.

flower

BALACLAVA HELMET
Pattern, page 55.

Fold the faceband in half lengthwise. With right sides together, stitch the band around the face opening of helmet with seam allowances toward the face, creating an edge for flower. Hotglue each two petals together, stuffing lightly with fiberfill. Arrange the straight ends of petals all around one of the rings, spacing evenly, and hotglue. Hotglue the second ring on top, stuffing lightly. Hotglue the finished flower to the helmet.

GOWN

Stitch sleeves to bodice. Stitch sides and underarms. Sew wide bias binding around neck for a casing and insert elastic. Hem sleeve ends and lower edge. Cut stem and leaves from orange fabric and hotglue to front.

NO-SEW SHORTCUT
Polarfleece gown, pattern, page 19.

Decorate as shown. Hotglue everything.

TREAT BAG
Pattern, page 71.

Cut a large flower from orange fabric and hotglue to the bag.

WHAT YOU NEED (FLOWER)

Size (approximate age in years)→	Small (3-4)	Medium (6-8)	Large (10-12)
Green medium-weight cotton-type fabric for gown, 55" (140cm) wide:	1¾ yds. (1.60m)	2¼ yds. (2.10m)	3¼ yds. (3.00m)
Green Polarfleece for balaclava helmet and faceband, 60" (150cm) wide:	½ yd. (0.50m)	½ yd. (0.50m)	½ yd. (0.50m)
Orange Polarfleece for flower and decorations, 60" (150cm) wide:	1 yd. (1.00m)	1 yd. (1.00m)	1 yd. (1.00m)

Other supplies:
- ❏ polyester fiberfill
- ❏ leftover fabrics for treat bag
- ❏ wide bias binding for neck edge
- ❏ hot glue gun and glue sticks
- ❏ narrow elastic for neck edge

BALACLAVA HELMET
Pattern, page 55.

Cut a pile of simple leaves from felt. Starting at the bottom of the helmet and attaching only the upper stem ends, hotglue the leaves all over.

CAPE

Cut a large circle for a cape. Cut out a neck opening. Cut a huge pile of simple leaves from felt. Hotglue the leaves to cover the entire cape as for helmet.

TREAT BAG
Pattern, page 71.

Draw a simple tree on the paper backing of fusible web. Iron it behind dark fabric, cut out, peel off the paper, and fuse the design onto the bag. Add a few colorful leaves.

WHAT YOU NEED (TREE)

Brown Polarfleece for cape and balaclava helmet, 60" (150cm) wide:

Size (approximate age in years)		
Small (3-4)	**Medium (6-8)**	**Large (10-12)**
1 yd. (1.00m)	1¼ yds. (1.20m)	1¼ yds. (1.20m)

Other supplies:
- ❑ large assortment of felt squares in fall colors
- ❑ hot glue gun and glue sticks

For treat bag and decorations:
- ❑ fabric
- ❑ fabric scraps
- ❑ paper-backed fusible web

Enlarging grid patterns, page 13.
Using hot glue, page 14.

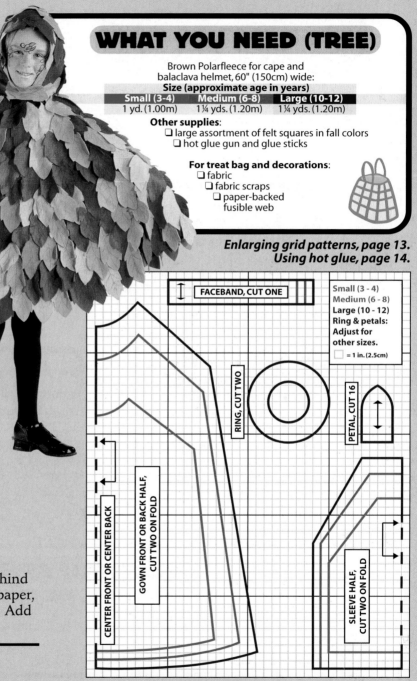

FACEBAND, CUT ONE

Small (3 - 4)
Medium (6 - 8)
Large (10 - 12)
Ring & petals:
Adjust for other sizes.

☐ = 1 in. (2.5cm)

RING, CUT TWO

PETAL, CUT 16

CENTER FRONT OR CENTER BACK

GOWN FRONT OR BACK HALF, CUT TWO ON FOLD

SLEEVE HALF, CUT TWO ON FOLD

Corn-On-The-Cob

Corn is the only native American cereal grain. Originating in Central America or Mexico, it was used by pre-Columbian civilizations as a staple food, currency, fuel, and construction material for thousands of years. Corn and its silky threads were also utilized in making jewelry and tobacco. The delicious kernels are borne on long ears on a robust annual plant.

BALACLAVA HELMET
Pattern, page 55.

Use leftover fabric to roll up a thick stem-end and hotglue to the helmet top. Cut leaves from Polarfleece and hotglue around the stem.

KERNELS

Cut circles from yellow Polarfleece. Using a long needle and strong thread, hand-baste all around the edge and pull the thread to create a pouch. Stuff lightly with fiberfill and handsew closed. Hotglue the kernels to tabard front.

TABARD
Pattern, page 61.

Hotglue the shoulder seams. With wrong sides together, hotglue front to back along the right side seam. Sew pieces of Velcro or ties to attach the left side seam.

COLLAR WITH GIANT LEAVES

Hotglue shoulder seams. Handsew a piece of Velcro for front closure. Cut giant leaves from green Polarfleece. Arrange the leaves on top of the collar at sides and back. Hotglue in place at top edge only.

WHAT YOU NEED

Size (approximate age in years)→	Small (3-4)	Medium (6-8)
Green Polarfleece for balaclava helmet, tabard, collar, and large leaves, 60" (150cm) wide:	2 yds. (1.80m)	2¼ yds. (2.10m)
Yellow Polarfleece for large kernels, 60" (150cm) wide:	¾ yd. (0.70m)	¾ yd. (0.70m)

Other supplies:
- ❏ one bag of polyester fiberfill for kernels
- ❏ long needle and strong thread
- ❏ Velcro for tabard and collar closure, ½ yd. (0.50m)
- ❏ hot glue gun and glue sticks

For treat container:
- ❏ large empty bleach bottle
- ❏ Polarfleece scraps

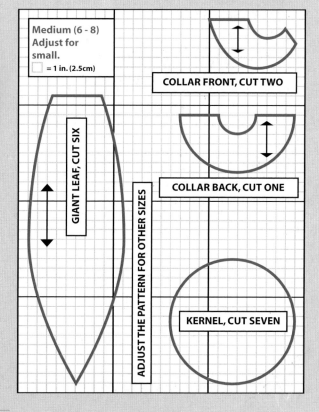

TREAT CONTAINER

Wash a large bleach bottle thoroughly. Cut off the top. Cut a narrow strip from rim for a handle. Hotglue brown Polarfleece over the container and handle. Hotglue the handle in place. Make tiny yellow pompoms from leftover scraps (see page 91). Hotglue the pompoms to the container and add a few green Polarfleece leaves as shown.

Enlarging grid patterns, page 13.
Using hot glue, page 14.

Medium (6 - 8)
Adjust for small.
☐ = 1 in. (2.5cm)

COLLAR FRONT, CUT TWO

GIANT LEAF, CUT SIX

ADJUST THE PATTERN FOR OTHER SIZES

COLLAR BACK, CUT ONE

KERNEL, CUT SEVEN

Pumpkin

The great pumpkin has emerged as the single most popular symbol of Halloween. Decorating houses, windowsills, and front entrances, it is a signal to trick-or-treaters that they are welcome.

BALACLAVA HELMET

Stitch or hotglue center front and center back seams.

DECORATE THE HELMET

Roll up a piece of brown Polarfleece as a stem-end and hotglue to helmet top. Cut simple leaves from Polarfleece in two shades of brown. Hotglue the upper ends to helmet around the stem-end. Cut long, narrow strips from brown Polarfleece across the stretchy width and pull into curly strings. Hotglue upper ends to helmet top, letting lower ends trail off freely.

WHAT YOU NEED

Size (approximate age in years)→	Small (3-4)	Medium (6-8)
Black Polarfleece for tabard, balaclava helmet, and facial features of Pumpkin, 60" (150cm) wide:	1¼ yds. (1.20m)	1⅓ yds. (1.30m)
Orange Polarfleece or felt for pumpkin face, 60" (150cm) wide:	⅝ yd. (0.60m)	¾ yd. (0.70m)
Two different shades of brown Polarfleece for helmet trimmings, 60" (150cm) wide, each:	¼ yd. (0.25m)	¼ yd. (0.25m)

Other supplies:
- ❏ one bag of polyester fiberfill
- ❏ Velcro for tabard closure
- ❏ needle and thread
- ❏ hot glue gun and glue sticks

For treat container:
- ❏ large plastic pumpkin
- ❏ orange Polarfleece
- ❏ brown Polarfleece scraps

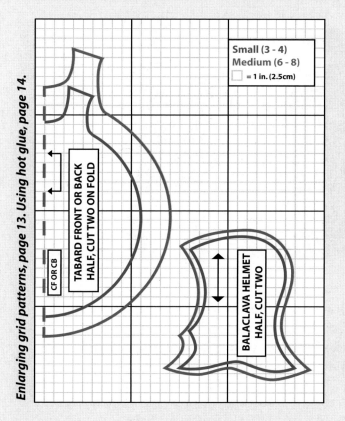

Enlarging grid patterns, page 13. Using hot glue, page 14.

Small (3 - 4)
Medium (6 - 8)
☐ = 1 in. (2.5cm)

CF OR CB

TABARD FRONT OR BACK
HALF, CUT TWO ON FOLD

BALACLAVA HELMET
HALF, CUT TWO

TABARD

Hotglue the shoulder seams. With wrong sides together, hotglue front to back along the right side seam. Sew pieces of Velcro or ties to attach the left side seam. Cut two large circles from orange Polarfleece for pumpkins, trim to match the tabard, and hotglue around edges to the tabard front and back. On inside, cut a small slit at chest level of black Polarfleece only, front and back. Push a few handfuls of fiberfill through the slits. Cut simple facial features from black Polarfeece and hotglue to front as shown.

TREAT CONTAINER

Hotglue orange Polarfleece over a plastic pumpkin and handle. Decorate with leaves and curly strings to match the helmet.

Costumes are not just for Halloween. Children love playing dress-up games all year round. A box filled with a few costumes and accessories, along with discarded clothes and other simple supplies, will spark their imagination for endless fantasy play.

Last-Minute Panic Solutions

It's five minutes to Halloween and your child needs a costume... These no-sew costumes are so fast and easy that older children can make them. Keep ordinary supplies on hand such as posterboard, construction paper, markers, poster paints, old clothes and hats, pieces of white and colorful fabrics, gift wrap and gift tissue, costume jewelry, vinyl sheets, aluminum foil, string, safety pins, corks, bottle caps, glue, double-sided foam tape, and duct tape. If you have some time, thrift shops and flea markets are interesting hunting grounds. With proper supplies, it takes just minutes to improvise a quick costume even if you don't have time to plan it in advance or to go shopping.

ARTIST

- ❑ A beret or a scarf tied around head.
- ❑ An old white shirt, stained with colorful poster paints.
- ❑ Cardboard palette with poster paint spots, attached to a tote with double-sided foam tape.
- ❑ Tie a colorful scarf around neck.

LADY

- ❑ Fancy old hat (look in thrift shops or flea markets).
- ❑ Grown-up dress tied at waist with belt. Sleeves and hem temporarily shortened.
- ❑ Costume jewelry, grown-up makeup.
- ❑ Lovely shawl draped on shoulders. Pretty purse.

CHEF

- ❑ PJ's or pants and white shirt.
- ❑ Fold and pleat tea towels or paper to form a chef's hat. Use safety pins or adhesive tape to fasten.
- ❑ Tie a scarf or towel and measuring spoons around neck.

DOCTOR

- ❑ Novelty store props such as toy stethoscope and headlight.
- ❑ The uniform is an old white shirt.
- ❑ Thermometer and tongue depressor (toys or cardboard versions) in pocket.

PARTY CRACKER

- ❏ Cut a body tube from corrugated cardboard. Cut out armholes and punch holes at back edges for strings.
- ❏ Use duct tape to attach ruffled gift wrap to upper and lower edges. Add decorations from gift wrap, etc.
- ❏ Tie child's hair into a dozen silly pigtails.

NURSE

- ❏ Make a cap from white cardboard.
- ❏ An old white shirt and belt. Shorten sleeves temporarily.
- ❏ Attach a white cardboard square to a tote. Cut crosses from red paper. Attach them to tote, pocket, and cap.

FLOWER CHILDREN

- ❏ Retro clothes and supplies from thrift shops and novelty shops.
- ❏ Wear jeans. Cut two curved pieces from flowered or striped fabric. Tape or baste them below knees to make bell-bottoms.
- ❏ Billowy blouse. Quilted, crocheted vest or jean vest.
- ❏ A floppy hat.
- ❏ Long necklace with peace symbol. Crocheted friendship bracelets.
- ❏ Tie a bandanna or scarf around one knee and a long cord around head over the hair.
- ❏ Add makeup of sixties with pale pink lipstick.

CANDY MONSTER

☐ Wear turtleneck and leggings or pants. For a poncho, cut a large circle from an old shower curtain, disposable table cloth, or old fabric. Cut out a neck opening.

☐ Use double-sided foam tape to attach wrapped candies all over the poncho and on headband or hat. Use real candy or fill used candy wrappers with wads of paper.

MISFIT

☐ Compete with friends for the silliest outfit from castoff clothes and toys. Anything goes.

☐ Stuff a sleeve from a discarded jacket for an extra arm. Cut off or roll up one pant leg, wear mismatched socks and shoes, a glove on one hand, a sock on the other.

TECHNOJUNKIE

☐ Make a body tube from cardboard. Attach edges at back with duct tape. Decorate with high-tech images (futuristic cars, computers, cell phones, spaceships, robots, rockets, web names).

☐ Shape crinkled aluminum foil into a helmet. Add antennas from pipe cleaners. Wear the helmet over a knit cap for added comfort.

EMAIL

☐ Wear long sweatshirt and leggings or pants. Cut two large circles from white posterboard, one for front, one for back. Add holes for strings to tie at shoulders and sides.

☐ With black marker, draw a huge @-symbol on center front and back.

☐ Tuck rolled-up emails under elastic headband.

SPIDER

❑ Cut two large circles from white posterboard, one for front, one for back. Add holes for strings to tie at shoulders and sides.
❑ Draw a spider's web with black marker. Draw a few fat spiders. Or make the spiders from construction paper or tissue paper and pipe cleaners.

ACCIDENT VICTIM

❑ Wrap a towel or piece of fabric around head and one leg. Attach with safety pins.
❑ Fold a large piece of fabric into a triangular bandage and tie it behind the neck for a sling.
❑ Paint scars on face with lipstick and brow pencil.
❑ Splash some Tabasco sauce or food coloring on bandages for blood stains.

BIG BABY

❑ Wear tights and bodysuit under this costume.
❑ Get props from novelty stores such as oversized pacifier, rattle, and baby toys.
❑ Bonnet or shower cap and baby's bib. For a diaper, attach a white towel with safety pins.

STOCK BROKER

❑ Cut two large squares from white posterboard, one for front, one for back. Add holes for strings to tie at shoulders and sides.
❑ Use a black marker to add grid and stock market symbols on the boards.
❑ Tape stock symbols all over a baseball cap.

TAXI

❏ Use yellow posterboard to cover a box and to make wheels, hat, and a big bow tie. Attach the wheels with glue or tape. Staple or hot glue hat together, and add elastic chinstrap. Decorate with black permanent marker as desired.

❏ Attach suspenders made from wide ribbon, crossed at back, to the box, using duct tape.

OLD WOMAN

❏ An old, adult-style jacket or coat. A large fringed scarf tied around shoulders. An old purse for treats.

❏ A scarf tied on head under the chin.

❏ Spectacles on nose tip (remove lenses from old sunglasses or make the frames from flexible floral wire).

SNIPS

❏ Snips, the alien kid, wears a hat made from a disposable aluminum pie plate. Twist antennas and hair from crinkled aluminum foil. Add chinstrap.

❏ For a poncho, cut a large circle from an old shower curtain or disposable tablecloth. Cut out a neck opening. Cut lower edge as shown. Add decorative details.

GHOST WINDOW

❏ Cut two large squares from posterboard. Add holes for strings to tie at shoulders and sides.

❏ Add ghosts from craft foam or construction paper, curtains from tissue paper or fabric, and a pumpkin from orange craft foam or construction paper.

VAGABOND

- ❏ Halloween Hobo wears old ragged clothes and a floppy hat with a flower. Add patches from fabric scraps or paper.
- ❏ Smear black makeup on chin and cheeks.
- ❏ Tie a big scarf into a bundle and attach it to a stick.

HALLOWEEN CLOCK

- ❏ Cut two large circles from orange posterboard, one for front, one for back. Add holes for strings to tie at shoulders and sides.
- ❏ Replace hour numbers with holiday symbols such as a turkey for Thanksgiving and a heart for Valentine's Day, made with craft supplies and markers. Add a big arrow, pointing it to the pumpkin as the Halloween symbol.

MARTIAN

- ❏ A colander becomes a helmet. Attach foil or wire antennas and elastic chinstrap with duct tape.
- ❏ A breast plate from stiff cardboard is covered with foil or paper. Glue corks and bottle caps to front. Add strings to tie at back.

GIFTBOX

- ❏ Remove top from a large cardboard box. Turn the box upside down. Cut out holes for head and arms.
- ❏ Glue gift wrap or comic pages all around the box. Cut wide strips from fabric or gift wrap and glue around the box for ribbons.
- ❏ Attach a huge ribbon bow to a hairband on top of child's head.

Glossary

BIAS TAPE A strip of lightweight fabric, cut on the bias for flexibility, and prefolded for ease of use. Use bias tape to trim cut edges and to sew casings for elastic around neck edges. (Consider making your own version by cutting a fabric strip on the bias and pressing it folded as needed.)

FUSIBLE WEB Translucent, heat-activated, mesh fabric adhesive. When pressed with a hot iron, it bonds together fabric layers. It is especially useful for bonding thin fabrics and fusing hems. Ready-made web strip is also available. (See page 15.)

FUSIBLE WEB WITH PAPER BACKING Indispensable for two-step fusing of small intricate designs. A design is drawn on the paper backing, ironed to the wrong side of appliqué fabric, cut out, and the paper backing peeled off. The design is then fused to the fabric with a medium-hot iron. (See page 15.)

GALVANIZED WIRE Available in hardware stores, it comes in several thicknesses. The designs in this book require 16-gauge wire which is flexible yet sturdy enough for wings and stiff hemlines. (Consider using a wire coat hanger or stiff floral wire as a substitute when practical for antennas, etc.)

HOT GLUE GUN An electric tool shaped like a gun available in hardware and craft stores along with glue sticks. It melts glue sticks and when the trigger is pulled, dispenses hot liquid glue that bonds almost immediately and dries fast. A hot glue gun is essential for many costumes in this book. (See page 14.)

POLARFLEECE, ARCTIC FLEECE, POLYESTER FLEECE Polarfleece® is the best-known and commonly used registered trademark for arctic fleece or polyester fleece (also known as polar, fleece, or high loft fleece). It is an ideal fabric for children's Halloween costumes. Soft and lightweight, slightly stretchy, warm and comfortable, it comes in dozens of colors and prints. Relatively inexpensive and conveniently wide, it hotglues well and won't ravel. (See page 14.)

POLYESTER FIBERFILL Soft and lightweight, a bulky fiber sold by the bag. It is used to stuff tabards, animal ears, pompoms, octopus arms, etc.

TABARD A shell-like outer garment worn over other clothing, is a practical base for many costumes (Snowman, Ladybug, Bumblebee, Sun & Moon, Corn-On-The-Cob, and Pumpkin). In this book, it consists of sleeveless front and back panels connected at the shoulders. One side is hotglued closed while the other side has Velcro or ties for easy closing. The surface is embellished with details. A lining or surface layer is sometimes added so you can stuff fiberfill in between the layers.

VELCRO Velcro® is a registered trademark for a hook-and-loop fastener tape. It comes with one tape of dense nylon hooks and another tape of dense nylon pile that interlock firmly when pressed together. It is fast and practical as a closure for helmets, tabard sides, and belts instead of buttons, zippers, snaps, ties, etc.

Index

Photo by Albert Albala

About the author

Leila Peltosaari Albala has been designing costumes for children for twenty years. She had never heard of Halloween before moving to Canada from her native Finland in 1973. Fascinated by costumed trick-or-treaters, she started making costumes for her own children, and wrote her first Halloween costume book in 1985. It became a perennial best-seller after being featured in hundreds of magazines and newspapers. Her own children are now grown, but new generations inspire her with their excitement over Halloween and costumes. Leila has also written other user-friendly, easy books on sewing, crafts, and cooking. She lives near Montreal in Quebec, Canada.

Need more copies?
Please use the order form
on the next page or
visit tikkabooks.com

Photocopy this order form as needed

Softcover, 142 pages,
ISBN 1-896106-03-X
U.S. $19.95 / CAN $29.95

CELEBRATE HALLOWEEN AND MAKE MEMORIES

Illegally Easy™ HALLOWEEN COSTUMES FOR KIDS
100 costumes with simple patterns, no-sew shortcuts, last-minute solutions, treat bags & accessories

Full-color photos and well-organized layout plans will guide and inspire you for many Halloweens to come. This exciting yet practical book is a treasure-trove of safe and comfortable designs for children of all ages. Most costumes can be made without a sewing machine in just one evening. Create an unforgettable original for a child. Just imagine the memories!

A portion of the proceeds from the sale of this book will be donated to UNICEF.

If you can't find this book at your favorite store, we offer a mail-order service for your convenience. Send orders to:
TIKKA BOOKS PO Box 203 Chambly Quebec J3L 4B3 Canada   Phone: (450) 658-6205 Fax: (450) 658-3514
www.tikkabooks.com   leila@tikkabooks.com   Quantity discounts available.

NUMBER OF COPIES	TITLE	USA ORDERS	CANADIAN ORDERS	TOTAL
	ILLEGALLY EASY ™ HALLOWEEN COSTUMES FOR KIDS	U.S. $19.95	CAN $29.95	

HALLOWEEN TREAT: FREE SHIPPING.
(GST INCLUDED FOR CANADIAN CUSTOMERS.)

SEND A CHECK OR CHARGE IT
TO YOUR VISA OR MASTERCARD

NAME _____   DATE _____

ADDRESS _____

CITY _____   STATE/PROVINCE _____   ZIP/POSTAL CODE _____

TELEPHONE NUMBER OR EMAIL _____

VISA/MC NUMBER _____   EXPIRY DATE _____   SIGNATURE _____

COMMENTS _____